Introduction

Mental health encompasses a person's emotional, social, and mental well-being. Many people struggle with their mental health and well-being, and there are multiple reasons for this. A person's family history, diet, home life, trauma, a substantial life change, etc., can all affect their mental health.

The initial pages of each topic include an explanation geared toward the parent or teacher. Terms are defined and tips for presenting the information to the students are provided. The student pages include brief descriptions of the topic and self-assessments, journaling, or other open-ended activities designed to get students thinking about their own experiences and feelings.

While mental disorders are nothing new, they are more prevalent today than ever before. Not only do more than 43 million Americans struggle with mental disorders, but Generation Z (people born between 1997 and 2012) are experiencing the highest amounts of anxiety and depression of any generation before them. The reasons for this are many—social media, the Coronavirus pandemic, the mainstream American diet, and more.

But fear not! There is hope and help provided in the following pages. In this book, mental disorders will be broken down into simple terms, and the reader will be provided with worksheets and tools to learn helpful ways to cope with and manage mental health concerns.

Parent/Teacher Page

Chapter 1: What Is Mental Health?

Mental health is more commonly talked about now than it has been in years past. There have been countless research studies that have looked in-depth into the causes, symptoms, and effects of mental disorders. Because of this, it has been discovered that **Gen Z** (people born between 1997 and 2012) is the most anxious and depressed generation the world has ever seen. While this is a daunting statistic, it is also a reminder that these young people are seldom alone when struggling with their mental health.

Because mental health is more readily discussed in today's society, that also means there is less of a **stigma** (a mark of shame toward a circumstance or quality) surrounding mental disorders. In previous generations, mental disorders were considered to be a combination of a hoax and someone being "crazy." It is now more readily understood that mental disorders should be regarded and treated like any physical illness would be. For example, if a child fell and broke their arm, it is not a question that medical attention would be necessary. In the same sense, if a child endures something traumatic or makes it known to you that their mental health is struggling, professional help should be sought out in the form of a therapist, psychiatrist, physician, etc.

Defining Mental Health

So, what exactly is **mental health**? According to mentalhealth.gov, "Mental health includes our emotional, psychological, and social well-being. It affects how we think, feel, and act. It also helps determine how we handle stress, relate to others, and make choices. Mental health is important at every stage of life, from childhood to adolescence through adulthood." It is also important to understand and remember that mental health struggles are often invisible and can easily go unnoticed by the people not experiencing them. For this reason, it is critical to intentionally check in on the people in your life—especially the younger people who are still learning how to vocalize their feelings and hardships. Many times, people may *seem* much happier or relaxed than they really are.

At this point, you may be wondering what causes mental disorders. A person's genetic makeup and a family history of mental disorders can be one cause. A change in one's brain chemistry, trauma, or a dramatic life change can all cause **dysregulation** with a person's mental health. In other words, the person has trouble regulating their emotional responses, such as sadness, anger, or frustration. A dramatic life change that could cause a young person to experience stress could look like…

- Parents separate/divorce/remarry
- Parent(s) job loss
- Parent(s) become ill
- Deployment of a parent in the military
- Death of a loved one
- Birth of a new brother or sister

Signs and Symptoms of Mental Disorders

There are many signs and symptoms that point to a mental disorder. Look for the following symptoms listed on the Student Page (page 3) to know when you should take action regarding someone's mental health. The worksheet following the student section can be used by the student to evaluate the state of their mental health.

Managing Anxiety & Mental Health
Coping Strategies for Teens

Author: Alexis Fey
Editor: Mary Dieterich
Contributor: Penni Ippensen, LCSW Therapist
Proofreaders: April Hawkins and Margaret Brown

COPYRIGHT © 2023 Mark Twain Media, Inc.

ISBN 978-1-62223-883-5

Printing No. CD-405082

Mark Twain Media, Inc., Publishers
Distributed by Carson Dellosa Education

Table of Contents

Student Page

Chapter 1: What Is Mental Health?

Defining Mental Health

So, what exactly is **mental health**? According to mentalhealth.gov, "Mental health includes our emotional, psychological, and social well-being. It affects how we think, feel, and act. It also helps determine how we handle stress, relate to others, and make choices. Mental health is important at every stage of life, from childhood to adolescence through adulthood." It is also important to understand that mental health struggles are often invisible and can go unnoticed by others. For this reason, it is important to learn how to talk about your feelings.

Mental disorders can be caused by a person's **genetic makeup** determined by their genes and **family history of mental illness**. A change in one's **brain chemistry**, **trauma**, or a **dramatic life change** can all cause **dysregulation** with one's mental health. This is when a person has trouble regulating their emotions, such as sadness, anger, or frustration. Examples of dramatic life changes that can cause stress for young people are when parents separate/divorce/remarry, parent(s) experience a job loss, parent(s) become ill, deployment of a parent in the military, death of a parent(s), or the birth of a new brother or sister.

Signs and Symptoms of Mental Disorders

There are many signs and symptoms that could point to mental health struggles. To know when your own mental health or that of someone you know needs your attention, it is important to look for the following symptoms:

- Trouble falling asleep and/or staying asleep; also sleeping too much
- Eating too much or too little
- Feelings of hopelessness, helplessness, or frequent sadness
- Wanting to be alone/isolate often
- Yelling or fighting with friends
- Mood swings
- Hearing voices that are not your own
- Intrusive thoughts (things that you don't want to think about, but cannot get out of your head)
- Thoughts of harming yourself or others
- Having little to no energy
- Feeling unusually and/or excessively confused, forgetful, on edge, angry, upset, worried, or scared
- Long-lasting sadness or irritability
- Dramatic changes in eating and/or sleeping habits
- Thinking your mind is controlled or out of control
- Use of alcohol or drugs to cope
- Hurting other people or destroying property

The following worksheet can be used to evaluate the state of your mental health.

Chapter 1: What Is Mental Health?

How Am I Feeling Today?

Label the statements below using the following ratings:

1 – Never   2 – Sometimes   3 – A lot of the time   4 – Almost always/always

_____ I feel sad.

_____ I feel like things will never get better for me.

_____ I am unhappy.

_____ I am angry with others.

_____ I yell at my family or friends.

_____ I have trouble sleeping at night.

_____ I sleep more than 12 hours a day.

_____ I want to hurt myself.

_____ I want to hurt others.

_____ I want to be alone.

_____ I have little to no energy and cannot get things done.

_____ I am worried that something bad will happen to me or someone I love.

_____ I keep thinking about things that I don't want to think about.

_____ My mood frequently changes and is all over the place. I will go from happy, to sad, to angry, to happy, to nervous, etc.

_____ I hear voices that are not mine.

_____ I don't want to be around my family/friends anymore.

_____ I feel excessively nervous and on-edge.

_____ I am confused and forget things more than normal.

_____ I feel numb or apathetic.

_____ I feel tense, anxious, and like I cannot sit still.

_____ I feel I must repeat certain tasks or rituals (counting or checking and re-checking things).

Student Page

Chapter 1: What Is Mental Health?

How Am I Feeling Today?

Action to Take:

If you have just one or more items that are concerning to you, you should talk to someone you trust. You can even use this page to show the person you have chosen if that will help you communicate what you are feeling.

Below, list some people you can trust and would be comfortable talking to if needed.

_____   _____

_____   _____

_____   _____

If you do not have a person that you trust to have this conversation with, that is okay! The **National Alliance on Mental Illness (NAMI) HelpLine** is here to help you. You can call or text them anytime at 1-800-950-NAMI (6264) or email them at info@nami.org. HelpLine volunteers will answer your questions and help you determine the next step in this journey. You can also visit their website, www.nami.org, for more information.

Parent/Teacher Page

Chapter 2: Communicating With Others About Your Mental Health

Why Communicating About and Caring for Your Mental Health Is Important

While it can be difficult to start the conversation, it is necessary to teach young people how to talk about their mental health, who they should have the conversation(s) with, and most importantly, why it is so beneficial to have these conversations. Remember that it can be scary and intimidating for them to come to you with these feelings, as it is for some adults, but when you lend a listening and non-judgmental ear, the conversation will be much easier for them.

Mental disorders affect much more than just your mental state. Being in a negative mental state can wreak havoc on your productivity, sleep, immune system, relationships, performance at work and school, and more. If not addressed and left untreated, mental disorders can worsen over time. As previously mentioned, think of treating mental health the same as you would when it comes to treating physical conditions. If a broken arm is left untreated, through the course of everyday life, it will worsen. The pain, risk of infection, and the bone's ability to heal properly will all be impaired. In the same sense, when mental disorders are left unaddressed and untreated, the symptoms and the person's ability to manage those symptoms will worsen over time. This can cause a child's school performance, social life, and family relationships all to suffer.

But the great news is that mental disorders don't have to get to that point—there are treatment options! Early intervention is key because the sooner a person gets help, the more effective the treatment will be. Also, not everyone is in need of professional treatment, such as therapy or medications prescribed by a doctor; some people just need to communicate to those closest to them that they aren't doing well. Talking about what they are going through and having a shoulder to lean on can be sufficient help in itself at times.

Group therapy is one form of treatment that can help with mental disorders.

Included is a worksheet that will guide young people on how to have this conversation and who they can talk to.

Chapter 2: Communicating With Others About Your Mental Health

Mental disorders affect much more than just your mental state. Being in a negative mental state can wreak havoc on your productivity, sleep, immune system, relationships, performance at work and school, and more. If not addressed and left untreated, mental disorders can worsen over time. Think of treating mental disorders the same as you would when it comes to treating physical conditions. If a broken arm is left untreated, through the course of everyday life, it will worsen. The pain, risk of infection, and the bone's ability to heal properly will all be impaired. In the same sense, when mental disorders are left unaddressed and untreated, the symptoms and the person's ability to manage those symptoms will worsen over time. This can cause school performance, social life, and family relationships all to suffer.

But the great news is that mental health disorders do not have to get to that point—there are treatment options! Early intervention is key because the sooner a person gets help, the more effective the treatment will be. Also, not everyone is in need of professional treatment, such as therapy or medications prescribed by a doctor; some people just need to communicate to those closest to them that they aren't doing well. Talking about what they are going through and having a shoulder to lean on can be sufficient help in itself at times. You could practice talking about your mental health by discussing the self-assessment on page 4 with a trusted individual or by completing the following activities.

Talking About Mental Health

Below are three scenarios to help you practice talking about your mental health. Read through the scenarios and answer the prompts accordingly.

Scenario 1: You wake up in the morning feeling exhausted because you tossed and turned all night, getting no rest. This happens often for you. You get to school and fight with your friends. Lunch comes and you have no appetite, so you decide not to eat. You can't focus in class all afternoon and just want to go home and lay under your covers. This is common and considered a normal day for you.

Should you talk to someone about how you are feeling? _____

If so, first write the name of the person(s) you could talk to.

Name _____ Phone number (if needed) _____

Write out what you would say to this trusted person to let them know you need help.

_____

_____

_____

_____

Student Page

Chapter 2: Communicating With Others About Your Mental Health

Talking About Mental Health

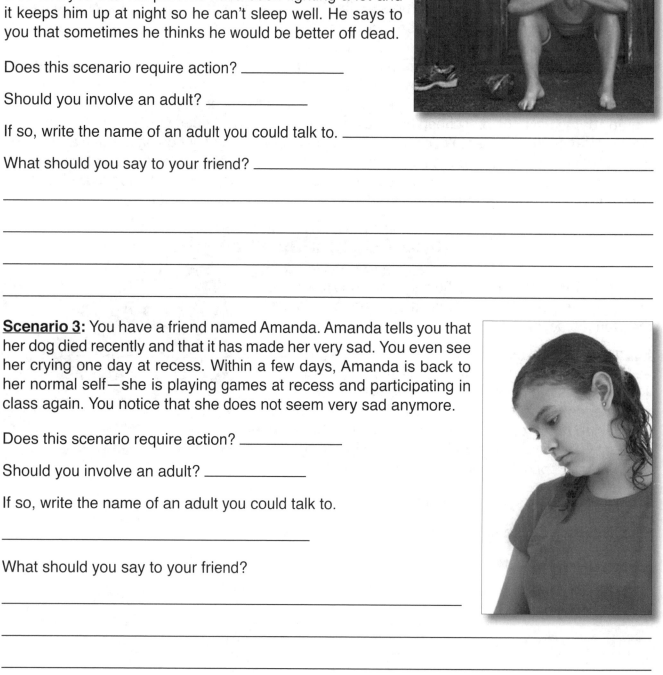

Scenario 2: You have a friend named Joe who is going through a rough time. He was recently dismissed from the basketball team, which was really upsetting for him. He also told you that his parents have been fighting a lot and it keeps him up at night so he can't sleep well. He says to you that sometimes he thinks he would be better off dead.

Does this scenario require action? _____

Should you involve an adult? _____

If so, write the name of an adult you could talk to. _____

What should you say to your friend? _____

_____

_____

_____

_____

Scenario 3: You have a friend named Amanda. Amanda tells you that her dog died recently and that it has made her very sad. You even see her crying one day at recess. Within a few days, Amanda is back to her normal self—she is playing games at recess and participating in class again. You notice that she does not seem very sad anymore.

Does this scenario require action? _____

Should you involve an adult? _____

If so, write the name of an adult you could talk to.

_____

What should you say to your friend?

_____

_____

_____

Parent/Teacher Page

Chapter 3: Common Mental Disorders

Anxiety

Anxiety is one of the most common mental disorders experienced by people today. Over 40 million adults and over 5 million children have a diagnosed anxiety disorder in the United States. However, not all anxiety warrants a diagnosis or is considered bad. In fact, a certain amount of anxiety is normal and should exist in a person's life. **Anxiety** is a feeling of worry or nervousness that is typically accompanied by increased heart rate, rapid breathing, sweating, etc. Anxiety is common when there is a big test approaching or when one has to speak in front of others, and it is this anxiety that motivates one to do well on such activities by studying for the test or rehearsing the speech. A certain amount of anxiety can also be helpful when someone finds themself in a dangerous situation, because anxiety can heighten the senses and trigger one's **fight or flight response**.

Anxiety can present itself in many forms. Most commonly, one will experience increased heart rate, rapid breathing, sweating, and racing thoughts. However, there are also symptoms of anxiety that vary from person to person. These symptoms might include heartburn, nausea, headaches, trouble sleeping, muscle and joint pain, etc. There are also "nervous tics" that people might experience such as biting of the nails, lips, and inside of cheeks, fidgeting, stuttered speech, and bouncing their legs when seated. Anxiety becomes concerning and might warrant a disorder diagnosis when its symptoms are persistent and long-lasting, triggered by something small or occur without a trigger, and when it inhibits one from focusing on and completing daily tasks.

Depression

Depression is a mood disorder that causes a persistent feeling of sadness and loss of interest in everyday activities. Depression can affect one's feelings, thoughts, and behaviors. It can also make day-to-day activities difficult to complete and make life feel like it is no longer worth living. The average age that a person first reports feeling depressed is 15 years old, and research has shown that women are twice as likely to experience depression in their lifetime as men.

While everyone's experience with depression is unique, some common symptoms include trouble sleeping, significant weight gain or loss, trouble focusing, thoughts of self-harm or suicide, feelings of hopelessness, social isolation, mood swings, and feelings of worthlessness. As you can see, depression is more than just feeling sad. These symptoms become concerning and may warrant a diagnosis when they last for a period of two weeks or more and cause significant distress in a person's life.

Parent/Teacher Page

Chapter 3: Common Mental Disorders

ADHD

ADHD stands for **attention-deficit/hyperactivity disorder**, and it is one of the most commonly diagnosed childhood mental disorders. An **attention deficit** is when a child has trouble staying on task and staying organized, and when they do not pay attention even when spoken to directly. You may also notice that the child daydreams or "zones out" often. **Hyperactivity** is when a child appears to have too much energy, which may look like constantly moving, fidgeting, tapping, talking, etc. At times this behavior may seem inappropriate, but children with ADHD find it incredibly difficult to resist moving, regardless of the social situation at hand.

Children with ADHD may be mostly inattentive or mostly hyperactive or show a combination of both. Regardless, ADHD can interfere with success in school and social relationships, connecting with others, and even simple daily activities. In a child or teen, ADHD may look like having routine difficulty completing everyday tasks such as getting ready to leave the house, getting ready for bed, sitting still in class, staying quiet during a test, etc. Children with ADHD may also have difficulty partaking in activities that require one to sit still and be quiet, such as independent schoolwork or reading.

Eating Disorders

Eating disorders are not a lifestyle choice or a diet taken too far. An **eating disorder** is a behavioral condition that can affect the physical, social, and psychological well-being of a person. Eating disorders cause chronic disturbances in eating behaviors and are often accompanied by distressing thoughts and emotions. Eating disorders did exist before social media, but social media has added to a national obsession with thinness. In fact, eating disorders most often affect women between the ages of 12 and 35. Social media is filled with unrealistic, photoshopped images that provide young impressionable minds with unrealistic standards of beauty, oftentimes leading to body dissatisfaction and an intense desire to be skinny.

There are three main categories of eating disorders—anorexia nervosa, bulimia nervosa, and binge-eating disorder. **Anorexia nervosa** is characterized by the person obsessing over losing weight and becoming dangerously thin. A person could achieve this by consuming very low amounts of food and/or abusing laxatives and diuretics. They may also exercise excessively. **Bulimia nervosa** is also called **binge-purge syndrome**, as the disorder causes the person to go through a repeated cycle of binge eating and **compensatory behaviors** (expelling of the food that was just eaten through vomiting and/or the abuse of laxatives and diuretics). **Binge-eating disorder** is similar to bulimia nervosa in that the person engages in repeated and frequent overeating; however, there are no compensatory behaviors or efforts to get rid of the food after the binges.

Parent/Teacher Page

Chapter 3: Common Mental Disorders

PTSD

Posttraumatic Stress Disorder, or **PTSD**, is a mental disorder that a person can experience as a result of enduring a traumatic event. A traumatic event could be the death of a loved one, threatened death of self, neighborhood violence, car accident, loss of a parent, being the target of a threat, being evicted from your home, severe injury, sexual violation, physical or emotional abuse, natural disasters, war/active combat, or, specific to this generation, a world-wide shutdown caused by a pandemic, a school shooting, etc.

The symptoms may include any combination of reexperiencing the traumatic event by way of dreams,

Experiencing a traumatic event like a house fire can cause PTSD.

nightmares, flashbacks, and/or intrusive thoughts; avoiding people, places, or things that serve as a reminder of the traumatic event; constantly being on high-alert, jumpy, and easily startled; and feeling guilty for surviving the event when others did not and/or feeling guilty about what they had to do to survive. The symptoms of PTSD may begin directly after the stressful event, but in some cases, the response to the trauma may not appear until months or years after the event. The symptoms of PTSD are often **intrusive**, meaning that they appear suddenly and without warning.

Dogs can be trained to comfort and assist those who experience PTSD symptoms.

Chapter 3: Common Mental Disorders

Anxiety

Feelings of worry or nervousness, often with physical symptoms such as increased heart rate, rapid breathing, tense muscles, and sweating. Anxiety becomes concerning and might warrant a disorder diagnosis when its symptoms are persistent and long-lasting, triggered by something small or occur without a trigger, and when it inhibits one from focusing on and completing daily tasks.

ADHD

Stands for **attention-deficit/hyperactivity disorder** and includes symptoms of trouble focusing, difficulty staying on task and paying attention, and impulsive behaviors. An impulsive behavior is something a child does quickly and without thinking. Hyperactivity is when a child appears to have too much energy. This may look like constantly moving, fidgeting, tapping, talking, etc.

PTSD (Posttraumatic Stress Disorder)

A mental disorder that a person can experience as a result of enduring a traumatic event. Symptoms may include re-experiencing the event (nightmares, flashbacks, etc.); constantly being on high-alert, jumpy, and easily startled; avoiding things that remind you of the event; and survivor guilt. Symptoms are often **intrusive**, appearing suddenly and without warning.

Depression

A mood disorder that causes persistent feelings of sadness and loss of interest in everyday activities. Symptoms may include thoughts of self-harm or suicide, hopelessness, social isolation, feelings of worthlessness, and persistent fatigue. These symptoms may warrant a diagnosis when they last for a period of two weeks or more and/or cause significant distress in a person's life.

Eating Disorders

A behavioral condition that can affect the physical, social, and psychological well-being of a person. Symptoms include chronic disturbances in eating behaviors, often accompanied by distressing thoughts and emotions. The three main categories of eating disorders are **anorexia nervosa**, **bulimia nervosa**, and **binge-eating disorder**.

Student Page

Chapter 3: Common Mental Disorders

Matching Activity

Directions: Use what you have learned to match the terms and definitions of common mental disorders below.

Terms

_____ 1. Anxiety

_____ 2. Depression

_____ 3. ADHD

_____ 4. PTSD

_____ 5. Eating Disorders

Definitions

A. A behavioral condition that can affect the physical, social, and psychological well-being of a person; symptoms include chronic disturbances in eating behavior, often accompanied by distressing thoughts and emotions

B. Disorder that includes symptoms of trouble focusing, difficulty staying on task and paying attention, and impulsive behaviors

C. A mood disorder that causes persistent feelings of sadness and loss of interest in everyday activities

D. Feelings of worry or nervousness, often with physical symptoms such as increased heart rate, rapid breathing, tense muscles, and sweating

E. A mental disorder that a person can experience as a result of enduring a traumatic event

What Can You Do?

Have you ever experienced any of these symptoms or seen a friend or relative going through some of these symptoms? Did you know what was happening? Did you know what to do to get help or give help? See the Treating Mental Disorders unit on page 52 and the coping skills on pages 56–58 for ideas of what to do to relieve symptoms and how to deal with these types of mental conditions.

Student/Parent/Teacher Page

Chapter 4: The Connection of the Body and Mind

The Scientific Connection

Before discussing the mind-body connection, we must understand the meaning of "mind" as it is meant in this book. The mind entails much more than just the brain. While the brain is the hardware, the **mind** consists of mental states such as thoughts, emotions, beliefs, attitudes, and images. One's mental states can occur with or without conscious effort; for example, we may have an emotional response to a situation without understanding why we are reacting that way. Your mind and body are in constant communication with one another.

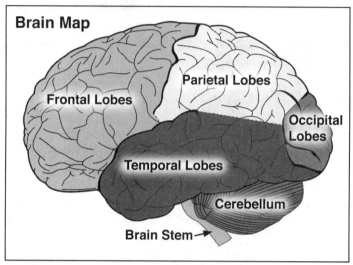

The brain is responsible for sending messages to your body to keep it functioning properly. For example, the brain is responsible for telling your heart to beat, your stomach to digest the food you eat, and your lungs to expand when you take a breath. The brain also releases certain chemicals, called **hormones**, that each play a different role in your health and well-being. They carry messages to different parts of your body through the bloodstream. Hormones are released into your bloodstream when different things happen to you, when you partake in certain activities, and when you feel a certain way.

The **pituitary gland** is responsible for releasing these hormones through your bloodstream, and it is located at the base of the brain right above the brain stem and behind the bridge of your nose. It is no larger than a pea, but it is an incredibly powerful structure. It is these hormones released by the pituitary gland in your brain that then travel through the bloodstream to various parts in your body that make up the **mind-body connection**.

Some hormones that are released by the brain produce feelings of happiness and promote physical wellness. There are four main "**happy hormones**" that your brain releases into your bloodstream, and different triggers cause the release of these hormones. For example, laughing and exercising release a hormone called an **endorphin** into your bloodstream that helps reduce pain and increase your mood and self-esteem. The four happy hormones are **oxytocin**, **serotonin**, **dopamine**, and **endorphins**. In this book, we will focus on dopamine and endorphins.

There are also hormones that are released by the brain that produce feelings of **anxiety**. The two main hormones that we will be discussing that produce feelings of anxiety are **cortisol** and **adrenaline**. These hormones might be released when something scary or nerve wracking happens to you, like a large dog barking at you or having to do public speaking.

In the following sections, you will learn the effects, both positive and negative, that food, exercise, rest, social media, relationships, trauma, and substance use have on the body and the mind.

Student Page

Chapter 4: The Connection of the Body and Mind

Fill in the Blank Activity

Word bank:

connection	cortisol	dopamine	happy
brain	messages	pituitary gland	endorphins
hormones	mind	adrenaline	

"Brain" and "mind" can mean different things—the _____ is similar to the hardware, and the _____ is made up of thoughts, emotions, beliefs, attitudes, and images. The brain is responsible for sending _____ to your body to keep it functioning properly. The brain also releases chemicals called _____ into your bloodstream that all play a unique role in your health and well-being. Hormones are released by the _____ _____, which is located at the base of the brain. It is the release of these hormones into your bloodstream and the effects these hormones have on your physical and mental state that make up the mind-body _____. The four main _____ hormones are oxytocin, serotonin, _____, and _____. Two hormones that cause anxious feelings are _____ and _____.

Parent/Teacher Page

Chapter 5: The Effects of Food on Your Mental Health

Over the last decade, there have been many studies that have come to a very important conclusion: **food is medicine**. We have known for a long time that what you eat impacts your physical health. It is now known that what is good for the body is also good for the brain. **Nutritional psychology** is an emerging field that reveals the effects of a person's diet on their mental health. Dr. Drew Ramsey dives into this topic in his book *Eat to Beat Depression and Anxiety* where he explains that there are three main things that are impacted by the food a person eats.

1. **Neuroplasticity** is the brain's ability to grow. Many used to believe that the brain stopped growing sometime in adolescence, but it was later discovered that the brain, when given adequate nutrients, can continue to produce new cells all throughout a person's life. This means that a person will never outgrow the need for a healthy diet.

2. **Inflammation** is how the body responds to stress. For example, redness and swelling may develop at the site of an injury. Once the injury is healed, the inflammation goes away. Inflammation can also be found inside the body in the cells and the brain. **Chronic inflammation**, or inflammation that lasts much longer than it should, has been linked to symptoms of anxiety and depression. The typical American diet that is low in fruits and vegetables and high in processed meats is directly linked to higher levels of inflammation and thus more anxiety and depression. A person whose diet consists of healthier whole foods, fruits, and vegetables is less likely to experience such symptoms.

3. **Gut health** is important, as it directly impacts the body's ability to digest foods. The "gut" involves the whole **gastrointestinal tract**, which includes organs such as the esophagus, stomach, and intestines. However, gut health also plays a major role in mental health. The gut and brain are in almost constant communication. The gut relies on the microbiome to relay the right information to the brain for optimal functioning. The **microbiome** is the complex ecosystem that lives within the gut and that is made up of trillions of microorganisms. What lives in the gut directly impacts not only the brain's ability to function well, it also impacts the chances of a person developing symptoms of anxiety and/or depression. The gut also secretes **hormones**. The gut is actually the largest hormone-secreting organ in mammals. In fact, the majority of **serotonin** neurons (one of the four happy hormones) live in the gut, not in the brain.

   The key to a healthy microbiome is diversity. Everyone is born with a microbiome filled with bacteria passed to them from their mother. After birth, every single interaction with the environment (petting a dog, trying new foods, shaking a strangers hand, etc.) can affect a person's microbiome. The body needs "good bugs" to help digest the food that is eaten and absorb the nutrients in that food. Even exposure to germs can help strengthen the immune system and gut health. **Probiotics** are good bugs that are often found in fermented foods like yogurt, sauerkraut, pickles, and kombucha. Having the right bacteria in the gut and a diverse microbiome improves the brain's ability to respond to and cope with stress.

HEALTHY GUT + DIVERSE MICROBIOME = HEALTHY BRAIN

Parent/Teacher Page

Chapter 5: The Effects of Food on Your Mental Health

In his book *Eat to Beat Depression and Anxiety*, Dr. Drew Ramsey also explores 12 main nutrients and 8 main food groups to focus on for optimal mental health. There are 12 main nutrients that every person should include in their diet to increase neuroplasticity, reduce inflammation, and improve gut health. **Nutrients** are chemical compounds found in food that are used by the body to function properly and maintain health.

12 Main Nutrients

1. Folate
2. Iron
3. Omega-3 fats
4. Magnesium
5. Potassium
6. Selenium
7. Vitamin A
8. Vitamin B_1
9. Vitamin B_6
10. Vitamin B_{12}
11. Vitamin C
12. Zinc

Fiber is also an important part of the digestive process. **Dietary fiber** is the part of plant foods that cannot be digested. Fiber helps clean out the colon, reduce cholesterol, and maintain blood sugar levels. And because a person feels full when they eat high-fiber foods, it helps maintain a healthy weight. Fiber is found in vegetables, fruits, whole grains, and legumes.

Many of the 12 nutrients might sound unfamiliar, but they can all be found in a variety of foods that can best be broken down into eight main food categories.

1. **Leafy Greens**

   This doesn't have to mean only salads. Leafy greens can mean pesto added to a sandwich, kale added to a smoothie, or spinach added to an omelet. You can also add greens to soups, pasta, and stir-fries. Leafy greens provide vitamin C, potassium, fiber, and magnesium. That's three of the 12 key nutrients plus fiber in just one food category!

2. **Rainbow Fruits and Vegetables**

   The old saying that you should "eat the rainbow" remains true today. Mother Earth provides so many colorful options to eat—like blueberries, oranges, strawberries, carrots, tomatoes, kiwis, grapes, raspberries, broccoli, brussels sprouts, dragonfruit, bell peppers, bananas, beets, olives, avocados, apples, cherries, watermelon, pineapple, onions, eggplant, sweet potatoes, grapefruit...the list goes on and on! Rainbow fruits and vegetables help fight off inflammation in the body and provide fiber, which is vital to gut health. Look for all the colorful options in the produce section of the grocery store or at the farmers' market. Also try to keep some frozen or canned veggies on hand, as these can be added to meals when fresh foods aren't available. At every meal, try to eat as much of the rainbow as possible.

3. **Seafood**

   Adding regular portions of seafood to one's diet can seem challenging, especially for people who live in more landlocked regions, but it does not have to be difficult. It can be as

Chapter 5: The Effects of Food on Your Mental Health

simple as swapping out the usual chicken or beef serving for some type of seafood. If fresh seafood isn't available, frozen or canned options work just as well. Try enjoying some fish tacos, salmon burgers, tuna salad, or shrimp and noodles. Seafood is packed with zinc, selenium, iron, omega-3 fatty acids, vitamin B_6, and vitamin B_{12}—that is HALF of the 12 key nutrients!

4. **Nuts, Beans, and Seeds**

The great thing about this category is how easy it is to incorporate in an everyday diet. Beans are often already included in soups and chilis, and nuts and seeds are the perfect on-the-go snack or addition to salads. Aim to include at least a small handful of these foods per day, no matter how they are eaten. This food group can provide magnesium, fiber, zinc, iron, and vitamin B_6.

5. **Meat**

This food category can be a point of controversy for some who stand firmly in the vegan and vegetarian camps. However, meat can be a powerful source of many vital nutrients such as iron, protein, and vitamin B_{12}. If possible, buying meat from local farms and ensuring that the animals are grass-fed versus grain-fed can make a huge difference in the sustainability and quality of the meat. Avoid or limit processed or deli meats, as these lack important nutrients and include salt and other chemicals that are not helpful to the body.

6. **Eggs and Dairy**

Once again, those who follow a vegan diet may avoid these foods. There are plant-based vegan alternatives. However, eggs and dairy are full of nutrients the body needs. Dairy, particularly fermented dairy like yogurt, helps keep our gut healthy and is a great source of protein and calcium. Choose dairy products carefully. Avoid yogurts flavored with artificial sweeteners and loaded with added sugars. Reduced-fat milks lack vital nutrients, and milk substitutes (almond milk, oat milk, coconut milk, etc.) are also often loaded with sugars and other harmful ingredients that defeat the purpose people try to accomplish by avoiding dairy. Eggs and dairy products can provide the following nutrients: B-vitamins, iron, zinc, selenium, and magnesium.

7. **Fermented Foods**

Fermented foods are important for a healthy gut and microbiome. This includes foods like kefir, yogurt, kombucha, and sauerkraut. The important component here is to watch out for added sugars and preservatives. For example, aim to eat plain yogurt with no added sugar and then add sweetness through honey and/or berries. Sauerkraut can be added to a salad to give it a little zing.

8. **Dark Chocolate**

Yes, it's true, chocolate is a part of a healthy diet! The key word, however, is *dark* chocolate. While it lands more bitter on the taste buds, it is much better for a person's physical and mental health. Dark chocolate can be a great source of potassium, fiber, protein, iron, zinc, and magnesium. Besides eating a plain dark chocolate bar, a person can also try adding cacao nibs to unsweetened yogurt or using cacao powder to make hot chocolate. When eating a plain dark chocolate bar, make sure it has only two main ingredients, cacao and sugar. Aim for a cacao content of 70% or higher.

Chapter 5: The Effects of Food on Your Mental Health

At some point in your life, you have probably been told to eat certain foods and avoid certain foods. While it is commonly known that fruits and vegetables are healthier than pizza and ice cream, it is important to understand why. The one thing to remember out of this entire section is that **food is medicine**. The food we eat plays a dramatic role in our physical and mental health.

There are three main things impacted by the foods you eat. **Neuroplasticity** is the brain's ability to grow throughout your lifetime. **Inflammation** is your body's response to stress. **Gut health** impacts your body's ability to digest foods, and what you put into your stomach directly impacts the hormones that are released into the rest of your body. Your gut is amazing and smart and plays a vital role in your physical and mental health without you even being aware of it.

Food has the power to make you feel groggy and sluggish, ultimately impairing your brain's ability to function well. On the other hand, food also has the power to make you feel alert and energized, improving your memory and ability to focus throughout the day.

As a child, your food choices are heavily impacted by your parents/guardians. The food that you eat is most likely the food that the adult(s) in your life has purchased and prepared. However, you can still take what you learn from this section and apply it to your life. If you want to make changes in your future food consumption, ask your parent/guardian to let you help with meal planning, to buy specific things for you, or ask to accompany them to the grocery store.

Listed below are some common foods that children like to eat that are generally unhealthy. Make note of the items on this list that you frequently enjoy, and be ready to see what you could replace these items with.

Common foods to avoid:
- ✓ Candy
- ✓ Chips
- ✓ Cookies
- ✓ Fast food
- ✓ Ice cream
- ✓ White bread
- ✓ Soda
- ✓ Cake
- ✓ Donuts
- ✓ Sugary cereal
- ✓ French fries
- ✓ Processed meats like hot dogs, bacon, and beef jerky

Unsweetened yogurt with fruit is a better choice than ice cream.

Student Page

Chapter 5: The Effects of Food on Your Mental Health

While avoiding these foods will help, it is also important to make sure you are eating the right foods, as this can improve your mood and decrease feelings of anxiety and depression. **Nutrients** are chemical compounds found in food that are used by the body to function properly and maintain health. There are 12 main nutrients that every person should include in their diet: folate, iron, omega-3 fats, magnesium, potassium, selenium, vitamin A, vitamin B_1, vitamin B_6, vitamin B_{12}, vitamin C, and zinc. Fiber is also an important part of the digestive process. **Dietary fiber** helps clean out the colon, reduce cholesterol, and maintain blood sugar levels. And because a person feels full when they eat high-fiber foods, it helps maintain a healthy weight. Fiber is found in vegetables, fruits, whole grains, and legumes.

Listed below from Dr. Drew Ramsey are the eight main food categories from which you should regularly try to eat.

8 Main Food Categories

✓ **Leafy Greens**
  • Examples: lettuce, kale, arugula, and spinach
  • Tip: Add spinach to an omelet or kale to a smoothie.

✓ **Rainbow Fruits and Vegetables**
  • Examples: apples, oranges, bananas, broccoli, blueberries, grapes, etc. The options are endless!
  • Tip: Try to eat something every day from every category of the rainbow— red, orange, yellow, green, blue and purple.

✓ **Seafood**
  • Examples: fish tacos, shrimp pasta, salmon burger, and cod filet
  • Tip: Try adding fish to a salad, sandwich, or pasta dish.

✓ **Nuts, Beans, and Seeds**
  • Examples: cashews, walnuts, almonds; sunflower seeds and pumpkin seeds; black beans, lima beans, and chickpeas

  • Tip: Add beans to soup or chili, eat nuts for a quick snack, or add seeds to a salad for a little extra crunch.

Chapter 5: The Effects of Food on Your Mental Health

✓ **Meat**
- Examples: chicken and beef from pasture-raised and grass-fed chickens and cows
- Tip: A grass-fed burger or chicken tacos are easy ways to consume meat.

✓ **Eggs and Dairy**
- Examples: eggs (be sure to eat the yolk!), unsweetened yogurt, and full-fat milk from pasture-raised cows.
- Tip: Try drinking one glass of full-fat milk per day.

✓ **Fermented Foods**
- Examples: yogurt, sauerkraut, and kombucha
- Tip: Unsweetened yogurt with granola and fruit makes a great breakfast!

✓ **Dark chocolate**
- Examples: cacao nibs, cacao powder
- Tip: Try adding cacao nibs to unsweetened yogurt or use cacao powder to make hot chocolate. Aim for dark chocolate with a cacao content of 70% or higher, as this directly impacts how good it is for you.

Whew! That was a lot of information to take in. If you are feeling overwhelmed, remember that it is okay to take it slow. Focus on adding a new food group to your family's diet each week, and have grace with yourself if it is harder than expected.

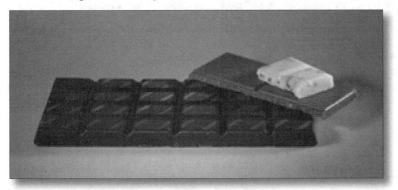

In the end, while it is important to avoid unhealthy, processed foods and to consume whole foods, remember that **fed is best**. If you, for whatever reason, do not have access to the healthier food options listed above, it is always better to feed yourself with what is available than to starve yourself.

Dark chocolate has more health benefits for you than milk chocolate or white chocolate.

Chapter 5: The Effects of Food on Your Mental Health

Food Diary

Directions: Fill out the food diary below for two days to track your current eating habits.

Day 1

	Food	Drink
Breakfast		
Lunch		
Dinner		
Snacks		

Day 2

	Food	Drink
Breakfast		
Lunch		
Dinner		
Snacks		

Student Page

Chapter 5: The Effects of Food on Your Mental Health

Goal Food Diary

Directions: Use the empty food diary template below to plan out how you could improve your eating habits. Take examples from the eight food categories listed on pages 20 and 21 and plug them into the food diary below to provide a goal eating plan.

Note: As a child/someone who does not live on your own, you are probably not buying your own food or preparing your own meals. If you would like to change your eating habits, ask your parent or guardian to let you help with meal planning. You can ask them to buy certain foods or ask to accompany them to the grocery store to apply what you have learned. Try to pick healthy items from the school lunch menu. If you feel limited by school lunches, try packing a lunch with food from home.

	Food	Drink
Breakfast		
Lunch		
Dinner		
Snacks		

Parent/Teacher Page

Chapter 6: The Effects of Exercise on Your Mental Health

It is commonly known that exercise is beneficial to one's physical health. When a person is regularly active, they will experience muscle growth and improvement in endurance. Exercise is also important because it provides the tissues, muscles, and brain with oxygen and keeps the cardiovascular system, digestive tract, and immune system all working optimally. When a person is intentionally taking care of their physical health, they are reducing their risk of chronic diseases like diabetes, heart disease, and lung disease. Clearly, the physical benefits are many, but that is not all! Exercise greatly impacts mental health as well.

As previously mentioned, physical and mental health are very closely related. For this reason, taking care of one's physical health will have a direct impact on one's mental health. Physical activity triggers the release of hormones called **endorphins**, which cause one to feel happy and experience improved memory and problem-solving skills. Endorphins also help block feelings of pain and discomfort, similar to morphine. Exercising also triggers the release of dopamine in the brain. **Dopamine** is another kind of hormone that the brain releases that causes one to feel proud and relaxed and experience improved memory and focus throughout the day. Increased levels of dopamine also help a person sleep better and have more energy throughout the day. Ultimately, the release of endorphins and dopamine help to decrease feelings of anxiety and depression, which is part of why it is so important for children to make this a habit while they are young. The more a person exercises, the easier it gets.

There are certain exercise recommendations that are provided by organizations such as the American Heart Association, the Centers for Disease Control and Prevention, and the Mayo Clinic. While any amount of exercise will be beneficial, the consensus is that children between the ages of six and 17 should participate in one hour every day of moderate to vigorous aerobic activity. This may seem like a lot of physical activity for a child to complete on a regular basis, but there are many practical and fun ways to implement exercise in the daily routine, including household and outdoor chores, team sports, individual sports and hobbies, exercise classes, free play, etc. Refer to the student section for a list of exercise ideas.

If a child is injured or suffers from a physical condition that makes exercise difficult, they should at least aim to spend time in direct sunlight. Sunlight exposure can also trigger the release of dopamine. On the contrary, a lack of sunlight can decrease dopamine levels, leaving one feeling generally down and sad.

Student Page

Chapter 6: The Effects of Exercise on Your Mental Health

The mind and body are closely related and are in constant communication with one another. It is widely known that exercise is beneficial to your physical health. For example, exercise helps provide your tissues, muscles, and brain with oxygen, as well as improving the function of your heart, lungs, and digestive system. In addition to benefiting your physical health, exercise also benefits your mental health.

When you take care of your body by providing it with exercise, the mind releases two main hormones into your bloodstream, **dopamine** and **endorphins**, which make you feel positive, happy, and relaxed. These hormones also help you sleep better at night and think more clearly throughout the day.

It is recommended that children between the ages of six and 17 exercise for at least one hour each day. While this may sound like a lot of exercise to complete, there are many practical and fun ways that you can incorporate physical activity into your daily routine. Also remember that the more you exercise, the easier it will be. Some ideas of daily physical activity are listed below.

- Walk your dog
- Walk with a family member/friend
- Yoga
- Pilates
- Mow the lawn
- Play outside with friends/siblings
- Rake leaves
- Ride your bike
- Rock climbing
- Hunting/fishing
- Horseback riding
- Gardening
- Hiking
- Participate in exercise classes through your local gym or YMCA
- Video games that encourage activity, like Wii Sports or Just Dance, which can be enjoyed alone or with family and friends
- Participate in team sports through school or local clubs
  - Baseball
  - Football
  - Soccer
  - Dance
  - Basketball
  - Volleyball
  - Lacrosse
- Participate in individual sports through school or local clubs
  - Martial arts
  - Track and field
  - Tennis

Chapter 6: The Effects of Exercise on Your Mental Health

- – Golf
- – Wrestling
- – Gymnastics
- – Skateboarding
- – Bodybuilding
- Participate in winter sports
  - – Skiing
  - – Snowboarding
  - – Figure skating
  - – Hockey
- Participate in water sports
  - – Water skiing
  - – Surfing
  - – Water polo
  - – Kayaking and canoeing
  - – Crew
  - – Swimming

If you are injured and unable to exercise, or if you do not have enough time one day, at least aim to spend time in direct sunlight. Sunlight exposure also triggers the release of hormones that make you feel happy and positive.

Incorporating Exercise Into Your Daily Routine Worksheet

List some activities below that you could do during recess or after school with friends to ensure your body gets the exercise it needs.

_____

_____

_____

_____

List some activities below that you could do during recess or after school by yourself to ensure your body gets the exercise it needs.

_____

_____

_____

_____

Parent/Teacher Page

Chapter 7: The Effects of Rest on Your Mental Health

Out of every topic discussed in this book, sleep is one of the most key factors in a person's overall health, and especially in a person's mental health. According to the author of *Why We Sleep*, Matthew Walker, "Sleep is the single most effective thing we can do to reset our brain and body health each day." However, despite teenagers needing 8–10 hours of restful sleep per night, a recent study from the Centers for Disease Control shows that two-thirds of high school students are getting on average seven hours of sleep or less on school nights. While studies on this subject are still emerging, evidence is beginning to show that sleep plays an active role in the sculpting of an adolescent's brain, which is actively developing until early adulthood. Instead of trying to discover what areas of a person's development are affected by sleep, researchers are now trying to discover if there is any area of development that is not affected by sleep.

Adequate sleep directly impacts a person's ability to problem-solve throughout the day. Sleep has also been shown to improve memory and a person's ability to learn and make logical decisions. Children who miss out on sleep often have trouble regulating their emotions and, therefore, exhibit bad behaviors. Sleep-deprived children will also have a hard time processing lessons in school and remembering new material.

When children experience frequent sleep disturbances, they are at a much higher risk of experiencing anxiety, depression, and suicidal thoughts. In the middle of the night, friends and family are not available to intervene in a crisis, and there is a general lack of other support. Missed sleep can already make a person feel dreadful, and it therefore makes everyday life feel more difficult as well. Sleep often provides temporary relief from life's struggles, so when a child misses out on that sleep, life can feel unbearable. Researchers have established a bidirectional relationship between sleep and mental health. This means that when one suffers, so does the other. Furthermore, when you treat one, you treat the other.

Children between the ages of 13–18 are recommended to get 8–10 hours of sleep per night. If your child has to get up at 6:00 A.M. to get ready for school, this means that they need to be in bed and asleep by 10:00 P.M. at the latest. This may mean going to bed between 9:30 and 9:45 P.M. This can be difficult for children who are involved in extracurricular activities after school and have schoolwork to complete at night. It is important for your teen to learn how to manage their time so that they can get to bed early enough each night.

To get good sleep, it is also important to know what can disrupt sleep, so that one can learn how to overcome the disruptions. Sleep troubles can greatly impact a young person's performance in school and sports and can affect their mood by making them feel irritable or depressed. So, what causes sleep problems in teenagers? Refer to the Student Page for a list of reasons a person might be struggling to get enough sleep.

To counteract sleep disturbances, check out the tips for getting a good night's sleep on the Student Page.

Parent/Teacher Page

Chapter 7: The Effects of Rest on Your Mental Health

Melatonin supplements are commonly used by parents because they think it will help their children sleep. Melatonin supplements, however, do not force a person to sleep. Melatonin is a hormone that everyone's brain already releases in the evening that makes them feel sleepy. Melatonin supplements were created mainly to assist people with sleep who are experiencing jet lag, insomnia, or **delayed sleep phase** (a sleep disorder that affects a person's natural circadian rhythm). Melatonin supplements were not created to give to children every evening just because parents want to make sure their children sleep through the night.

Melatonin can be dangerous to give children, as it is commonly not regulated by the Food and Drug Administration (FDA), meaning that companies that supply melatonin supplements can add as much or as little melatonin as they want, and as much or as little of other ingredients as they want. While short-term use of melatonin supplements is generally safe, long-term use of melatonin supplements can diminish the body's ability to produce melatonin on its own, thus forcing a person to be dependent on the supplement. Long-term melatonin side effects can include drowsiness, nausea, headaches, and dizziness. Melatonin supplements can also interfere with other medications and should be discussed with your primary care physician.

When a child becomes a teenager, they are most likely past the point of getting out of bed and finding an adult when they cannot sleep. It is important to intentionally check in with your teen and ask specific questions about how they are sleeping.

Student Page

Chapter 7: The Effects of Rest on Your Mental Health

Sleep is important in every area of a person's life and affects every aspect of their health, including their mental health. It is recommended that teenagers get 8–10 hours of sleep per night, even though research has shown that high schoolers are only getting an average of seven hours of sleep or less per night on school nights.

There is evidence that sleep plays a drastic role in the development of a person's brain, which continues to develop into early adulthood. Sleep contributes to a person's ability to problem-solve, memorize information, learn new things, and make good choices. Students who miss out on sleep often have trouble staying calm and keeping their emotions under control. They may become stressed out simply because they are too tired to process what is happening.

Sleep plays a vital role in a person's physical and mental health. On the physical side, insufficient sleep has been shown to increase a person's risk of developing cancer, Alzheimer's disease, cardiovascular disease, stroke, and congestive heart failure. Sleep also helps regulate a person's gut microbiome (also discussed in chapter 5) and overall body weight.

Regarding mental health, youth who experience inadequate sleep are at a higher risk of experiencing anxiety, depression, and suicidal thoughts. In the middle of the night, friends and family are not always available to intervene in a crisis, and there is a general lack of other support. Sleep often provides temporary relief from life's struggles, so when one misses out on that sleep, life can feel unbearable.

How much sleep should you be getting? Teenagers between the ages of 13–18 are recommended to get 8–10 hours of sleep per night. If you have to get up at 6:00 A.M. to get ready for school, this means that you need to be in bed and asleep by 10:00 P.M. at the latest. This may mean going to bed between 9:30 and 9:45 P.M. This can be difficult if you are involved in extracurricular activities after school such as sports and clubs and have schoolwork to complete when you get home. Learning how to manage your time so that you can get to bed early enough each night will be a key factor in getting enough sleep.

Sometimes, a person may be experiencing disrupted sleep without knowing why, which can make it difficult to counteract. Following are possible explanations for why a person may be struggling to get enough sleep.

- **Puberty** can cause a hormonal change that can affect sleep patterns and delay the time teenagers begin to feel sleepy. This is caused by the hormone **melatonin** being produced later in the night, which is what makes a teenager want to stay up later at night and wake up later in the morning.
- **Anxiety and stress** commonly cause poor sleep. Anxiety could be caused by nightmares, social problems, drastic life changes, or problems at school, to name a few.
- **Electronics** – the blue light that is omitted from electronic devices delays the body's release of melatonin, making it difficult to fall asleep and stay asleep.
- **Insomnia** is when a person has trouble falling asleep and/or staying asleep.
- **Restless leg syndrome** can disrupt sleep, since it is the sudden and irresistible urge to move the legs. Restless leg syndrome may also cause one to feel itching, cramping, tingling, or burning in the legs.

Student Page

Chapter 7: The Effects of Rest on Your Mental Health

- **ADHD** symptoms and medications used to treat ADHD may both disrupt sleep. People with ADHD also experience a later melatonin onset than their peers.
- **Nightmares**, which often accompany those suffering from PTSD, can easily disrupt sleep and make it difficult to fall back asleep.
- **Sleepwalking** can disrupt sleep, as the brain is partially awake during these episodes.
- **Sickness** can keep one awake at night simply because one is generally uncomfortable.
- **Some medicines** have side-effects that disturb sleep.
- **An uncomfortable sleeping environment** (too hot, too bright, etc.) can keep one awake at night.

To ensure that you are getting plenty of good, restful sleep each night, try the following tips.

- Establish a bedtime routine (see the following activity to help with this).
- Aim to go to sleep and wake up around the same time every day of the week. If you do want to sleep in, try not to sleep in more than one hour.
- Avoid napping at all if you can, but especially after 3:00 in the afternoon.
- Avoid caffeine, nicotine, and alcohol at any time of day.
- Set up a comfortable, quiet, and dark sleep environment.
- Exercise regularly (this will help your body be tired at the day's end), but not later than two hours before bedtime, as exercising too close to bedtime can keep you awake.
- Stop big meals 1–2 hours before going to bed (eating too close to bedtime can keep you awake because your body is hard at work digesting the food).
- Take time to intentionally relax before bed.
- Try to spend at least 30 minutes in natural sunlight sometime during the day, as this helps regulate your internal clock.
- If you have been lying in bed for 30 minutes and still haven't fallen asleep, get up and complete a relaxing activity such as reading or journaling. Do not use your phone or tablet or watch TV, as these things will wake up your mind even more.

- Only use your bed for sleeping. When you only sleep in your bed, your mind will associate your bed with falling asleep. If you watch TV, do homework, scroll social media, etc., in your bed, your mind will associate your bed with activities that keep you awake.

Melatonin supplements are commonly used today because people believe that melatonin will help them sleep. However, taking melatonin supplements can actually diminish your body's natural supply of the hormone. Supplements are commonly not regulated by the Food and Drug Administration (FDA) and can have long-term side effects, such as drowsiness, nausea, headaches, and dizziness. If you are struggling with getting enough sleep at night, talk to an adult to problem-solve, try the above-listed tips for good sleep, and avoid taking melatonin supplements.

Student Page

Chapter 7: The Effects of Rest on Your Mental Health

The Effects of Rest: Worksheet

Reflection:

What time do I usually go to sleep? _____ : _____ _____ P.M.

What time do I usually get up? _____ : _____ _____ A.M.

How many hours of sleep do I usually get in a night? _____ hours

What are some things that keep me from getting enough sleep at night?

_____   _____

_____   _____

_____   _____

Sleep goals:

How many hours of sleep do I want to get tonight? _____ hours

What time do I need to go to sleep tonight to help reach my sleep goal? _____ : _____ _____ P.M.

What time do I need to wake up in the morning to reach my sleep goal? _____ : _____ _____ A.M.

To help prepare your mind and body for sleep, you can start a bedtime routine.

Example bedtime routine:

- An hour before I go to sleep, I will stop eating. (Eating too close to bedtime can keep you awake because your body is hard at work digesting the food you just ate.)

- Half an hour before I go to sleep, I will turn off all electronic devices. (The blue light that is put off from these devices keeps your brain awake.)

- Right before I go to sleep, I will change into my pajamas and brush my teeth.

Your bedtime routine can look like this one, or you can create your own below.

An hour before I go to sleep, I will … _____

_____

Half an hour before I go to sleep, I will … _____

_____

Right before I go to sleep, I will … _____

_____

Chapter 7: The Effects of Rest on Your Mental Health

Sleep Diary

Use the following template to track how much sleep you get in one week. This will help you to see if you are sticking to your planned sleep schedule. If you have trouble getting enough sleep throughout the week, try adjusting your bedtime routine throughout the week.

My sleep goal is _____ hours per night.

Day of the week	Monday	Tuesday	Wednesday	Thursday	Friday	Saturday	Sunday
What time did you go to bed?							
What time did you fall asleep?							
How many times did you wake up during the night?							
What time did you wake up for the day?							
How many hours of sleep did you get last night?							
Note anything that interfered with your sleep last night.							

Parent/Teacher Page

Chapter 8: The Effects of Social Media on Your Mental Health

Just as it's important to feed your body the proper nutrients, it is also important to feed your mind the proper nutrients. Today, we live in a technological world that is constantly fighting for our attention, eagerly waiting to become the next thing we consume. Social media has become a part of everyday life for the vast majority of its users. Everything that you allow your mind to consume <u>matters</u>. Giving a child a smartphone is giving them far more than just a way to call friends and family. In today's world, a smartphone provides them with access to calling, texting, gaming, social media, TV shows and movies, messaging boards, news, videos, explicit content, and so much more.

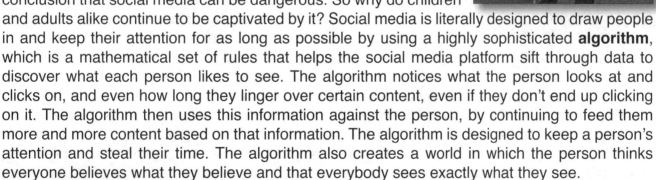

As of April 2022, there were 2.936 billion (2,936,000,000) total Facebook users, 1.96 billion of which use Facebook daily. Research has found that kids who are allowed to take their smartphone to bed are getting approximately one less hour of sleep when compared to children who are not allowed to take their phone to bed. Remember from Chapter 7 how vital sleep is to the young, impressionable, and developing brain. Studies continue to conclude that the more time a child spends on Instagram, the more anxiety they will experience. Astonishingly, five years ago, 62% of teenagers reported receiving at least one nude image on their phone, and 40% say they have sent one. Lastly, since the introduction of the smartphone, the suicide rate in students grades 8–12 has gone up by 65%.

These statistics are staggering and clearly point to the conclusion that social media can be dangerous. So why do children and adults alike continue to be captivated by it? Social media is literally designed to draw people in and keep their attention for as long as possible by using a highly sophisticated **algorithm**, which is a mathematical set of rules that helps the social media platform sift through data to discover what each person likes to see. The algorithm notices what the person looks at and clicks on, and even how long they linger over certain content, even if they don't end up clicking on it. The algorithm then uses this information against the person, by continuing to feed them more and more content based on that information. The algorithm is designed to keep a person's attention and steal their time. The algorithm also creates a world in which the person thinks everyone believes what they believe and that everybody sees exactly what they see.

People also continue to be addicted to social media because of the hormonal reaction that it causes in the human body. Every time a person receives a like or comment on something they post on social media, their brain releases a hit of dopamine. **Dopamine** is one of the four happy hormones that causes a person to feel pleasure. Dopamine is part of the mental reward system, encouraging the person to repeat whatever behavior they are exhibiting while feeling that pleasure. Comments and likes on posts act as positive reinforcement in that reward system, which makes social media incredibly difficult to stop using.

There are positives and negatives to every innovation, including the Internet and social media. The Internet has provided people with learning opportunities, access to health information,

Parent/Teacher Page
Chapter 8: The Effects of Social Media on Your Mental Health

organ donors, and connection to long-lost family members. However, when it comes to the Internet and social media, the cons have the potential to far outweigh the pros.

There are many dangers of social media. In a time where the Internet allows a person to "connect" with more people than ever before, humans are finding themselves more isolated, more anxious, and more depressed than ever before. Generation Z specifically is lonelier and more anxious than any other generation. Loneliness, as discussed in Chapter 9, is intimately related to serious mental health problems. Social media not only enhances but also feeds mental health problems. This is especially impactful to young people whose brains, sense of worth, and emotional intelligence are all still developing.

Refer to the Student Page for lists of the main dangers of social media usage and warning signs to look for when consuming social media. If you or your teen experience any combination of these symptoms, strongly consider taking an extended break from social media usage. You may need to consult with an expert on how to break the social media addiction.

Social media will not go away any time soon, so you should be aware of the steps you can take to cultivate a safe environment for the children in your life. **Intentional moderation** is key <u>if</u> you are going to choose to participate in social media. Most smartphones have the ability to limit the time spent on certain apps. You can turn this feature on to allow only one hour of social media usage per day, for example. If you are a parent, you can also turn off the WiFi in your house at night and during mealtimes to encourage everyone in the home to be present together. **Monitor** your teen's social media accounts with parental controls. **Explain what is unacceptable** when it comes to social media usage. For example, gossiping and spreading rumors, harassing others, and damaging another's reputation online are unacceptable behaviors. **Encourage in-person interactions** over online interactions. Remind your teen that connecting face-to-face will always be more fulfilling than an online connection. Finally, **spread awareness** with the teens in your life. Communicate with them why social media is dangerous so that they do not see your rules surrounding social media as unreasonable, but helpful and for their own good.

The average person spends five hours per day on their phone, adults included. Parents and teachers often sound frustrated with how frequently teenagers are on their phones. Remember that you have the power to take it away and put boundaries in place. Further, as important as it is for children to get off their phones, you, as the adults in their life, have the opportunity to set an example and lead them in this. Parents especially are in a unique position—they have the power to create bonding opportunities with their children to keep them off social media by simply spending intentional time with them. The child will feel infinitely more connected, seen, and cherished during that time of bonding than in countless hours spent on social media.

Student Page

Chapter 8: The Effects of Social Media on Your Mental Health

While it is important to feed your body the proper nutrients, it is also important to feed your mind with healthy content. Today, we live in a technological world that is constantly fighting for our attention. Social media has become a part of everyday life for many people, and everything that you allow your mind to consume matters. In today's world, a smartphone provides access to calling, texting, gaming, social media, TV shows and movies, messaging boards, news, videos, explicit content, and so much more.

Children and adults alike use social media so frequently because it is literally designed to draw you in and keep your attention for as long as possible. Social media use also causes a hormonal reaction in the human body. Every time you receive a like or comment on a social media post, your brain releases a hit of **dopamine**. This happy hormone is part of your mental reward system, and comments and likes on your posts act as positive reinforcement in that reward system. This makes social media incredibly difficult to stop using.

While some good things have come from social media, it can cause many dangers to your physical and mental health. Listed below are some of the main dangers of social media usage.

- **Cyberbullying and online harassment.** It is easy to be mean when you are hiding behind a screen. You forget that there is a real person with a heart and soul and feelings on the other side of that screen.
- **Exposure to explicit content.** Having a smartphone is having access to far more than just calling and texting. A smartphone allows access to unsupervised explicit content, which can lead to dangerous consequences, such as teaching young men to objectify women.
- **Enhanced struggles with self-esteem and social adjustment.** While teenagers are experiencing battles with self-esteem and social adjustment, they are simultaneously being exposed to diet culture, beauty and fashion trends, photoshopped and unrealistic pictures, etc. They are comparing their "b-roll" to everyone else's "highlight reel," and it can feel incredibly discouraging and demoralizing.
- **Peer pressure.** The pressure from social media can lead to teens following dangerous trends and experimenting sexually and with drugs.
- **Increase in mental health struggles.** There are children and teens who will wrestle with anxiety, depression, self-harm, low self-esteem, eating disorders, and suicidal thoughts because of their use of technology and social media.
- **Loneliness.** You may think you are getting "connection" by interacting with others on social media, but that is not true connection. The difference is that social media will always leave you feeling empty.
- **Disrupted sleep.** Not only are you tempted to stay awake with a smartphone in your bedroom, but the blue light that is emitted from these devices can also keep you awake at night.
- **Distraction from school and other responsibilities.** The addictive algorithm and social pressure of being on social media can easily distract you from other, more important things in life.

Student Page

Chapter 8: The Effects of Social Media on Your Mental Health

Listed below are warning signs to look for when consuming social media. If you experience any combination of these symptoms, strongly consider taking an extended break from social media usage. You may need to consult with an expert on how to break the social media addiction.

Physical symptoms
- Hand/wrist cramps
- Dry eyes and vision problems
- Neck/back problems

Mental and behavioral symptoms
- Trouble focusing on real life
- Discontentment with your own life
- Low self-esteem
- Feelings of isolation and disconnection
- Relying on social media as a constant form of entertainment
- Quickly judging others
- The persistent urge to check your phone, especially for likes and comments on your social media posts
- Automatically opening social media every time you open your phone
- Laziness and a general lack of energy
- Counting likes and comparing it to how many likes other people get
- Feeling the need to lie to others about how much you use your phone
- Constantly feeling left out of social situations
- Using social media as an escape to avoid or escape adverse moods
- Continuing to use social media despite having the symptoms mentioned above

Since social media will not go away any time soon, it is important to know how to safely consume social media. **Intentional moderation** is key if you are going to choose to participate in social media. Most smartphones have the ability to limit the time spent on certain apps. You can turn this feature on to allow only one hour of social media usage per day, for example. Understand what is unacceptable when it comes to social media usage. For example, gossiping and spreading rumors, bullying and harassing others, and damaging another's reputation online is unacceptable behavior. Remember that connecting face-to-face will always be more fulfilling than an online connection.

The average person spends five hours per day on their phone, adults included. If you are discouraged by how much the adults in your life are on their phones, share this information with them and encourage them to put their phones down. Do not let adults look down on you just because you are young; know that you can set the example for them if you feel compelled to do so. Finally, know that there is a life that you can live and experience with clear eyes and a full heart that is infinitely better than anything you could ever watch on a device.

Student Page

Chapter 8: The Effects of Social Media on Your Mental Health

Social Media Detox Activity

Monday	Tuesday	Wednesday	Thursday	Friday	Saturday	Sunday
Day 1 Delete unused apps from your phone.	**Day 2** Turn off push notifications.	**Day 3** Put your phone in a separate room at bedtime.	**Day 4** Unfollow people whom you aren't friends with, who bring you down, or who don't interest you.	**Day 5** No phone during mealtimes.	**Day 6** Don't check your phone until you've completed all your morning tasks (get dressed, eat breakfast, etc.)	**Day 7** Limit all social media apps to one 30-minute chunk of time in the day.
Day 8 Pick one social media app to avoid using for this entire day.	**Day 9** Put your phone away for two straight hours.	**Day 10** No phone until after school.	**Day 11** Pick a different SM app than the one you chose on day 8, and avoid it for an entire day.	**Day 12** Go somewhere and leave your phone at home.	**Day 13** No social media for an entire day.	**Day 14** No phone for an entire day.

If you find yourself struggling to make it through this challenge, here is a list of things you can do instead of getting on social media.

1. Go for a walk with family or friends.
2. Write down three things you are grateful for.
3. Bake a dessert.
4. Play a card or board game.
5. Read a book.

Use the lines below to think of five more activities you could do instead of getting on social media.

1. _____

2. _____

3. _____

4. _____

5. _____

Parent/Teacher Page

Chapter 9: The Effects of Relationships on Your Mental Health

Relationships are a key component of everyone's lives because humans are hard-wired for connecting with others; it is something we all need. Research has shown that people who have a higher number of strong social connections are happier and experience fewer mental health struggles when compared to those who have fewer/weaker social connections. Further, people who are more connected live a longer and healthier life. Essentially, regardless of how many relationships a person has in their life, they all play a role in that person's behavior, physical and mental health, and mortality risk.

Connectedness and the quality of those connections directly impact a person's health, partially due to the hormones that are released. For example, **oxytocin** is a hormone that is released by the brain and was discussed in Chapter 4 as one of the four happy hormones. Oxytocin is primarily released during almost any type of bonding or positive physical contact, like a deep conversation or a long consensual hug. Oxytocin promotes feelings of trust and empathy, and has been shown to lower stress and anxious feelings. People who are experiencing a release of oxytocin will feel a warm and fuzzy feeling around people they really love and care about.

Other benefits of strong social relationships include a stronger mental state and fewer struggles with mental health. Research from the UK has shown that regardless of what social class a neighborhood is in, those with more of a social community experience lower rates of mental health problems when compared with those of a lower social community. This means that strong relationships can help you keep a positive state of mind and suppress feelings of loneliness. Multiple scholarly studies have shown that the support of social relationships can drastically lessen, and even prevent, feelings of hopelessness, one of the main symptoms of depression and suicidal thoughts.

Loneliness and isolation are the opposite of connectedness and are breeding grounds for depression and suicidal thoughts. Loneliness has been shown to disrupt sleep patterns, heighten blood pressure and stress levels, and weaken the immune system. Loneliness has also been linked to an increased risk of obesity and can cause people to feel generally discontent. Further, when a person experiences loneliness for an extended period of time, it can lead to long-term health problems such as heart disease, stroke, and cancer. While diet, exercise, and sleep are all important aspects of a person's health, staying connected with friends, family, and the community also heavily contributes to living a healthy lifestyle.

Parent/Teacher Page

Chapter 9: The Effects of Relationships on Your Mental Health

The interesting thing about relationships is that they have the power to improve mental health struggles or enhance them, depending on how healthy the relationship is. In addition to loneliness, **negative and unhealthy relationships** can also have an adverse effect on a person's physical and mental health. Negative and unhealthy relationships might include relationships that are abusive or constantly have a lot of drama and conflict. If a friend or family member often lies or makes one constantly feel anxious and overall bad about oneself, that is not a healthy relationship.

Being in a relationship that is **toxic** and has a lot of conflict can be more damaging to one's mental health than being alone. Negative relationships can cause mental health problems like anxiety and self-esteem issues; in severe cases, negative relationships can be so traumatic that the hurt person is left feeling depressed and untrustworthy of any new person that tries to come into their life. For this reason, it is important to have boundaries and to know how and when to distance oneself from such relationships. Creating and enforcing boundaries can feel uncomfortable, especially if one does not like confrontation, but it is always worth it when someone is trying to protect and better their own mental health.

While unhealthy relationships should be avoided if possible, often there is a chance that a relationship can be healed and reconciled. Conflict resolution and forgiveness are two important skills that everyone should learn and practice throughout their life. **Conflict resolution** is necessary when two people are quarreling but want to remain friends. Conflict resolution happens when two disputing parties come to a peaceful solution by showing empathy, owning their own wrongdoing, and collaborating to reach a compromise.

Forgiveness has the tendency to be greatly misunderstood. People may think that because they have forgiven someone who has wronged them, that they are then being weak and condoning the wrongful behavior. However, true forgiveness is ultimately a shift in feelings and attitude toward an offense and the offender. The process of forgiveness involves a decision to overcome pain and to let go of anger, bitterness, and resentment (even though it may be justified).

However, if a relationship is **abusive**, steps need to be taken to leave the relationship and report the abuse to the proper authorities. This may involve telling a trusted person such as a parent, teacher, physician, or law enforcement officer.

It is important to encourage your teen to meet new people and make new friends, but also to work at keeping their existing friendships healthy. The handout at the end of this chapter will explain how to be a good friend, and the activity at the end of this chapter will allow the reader to practice conflict resolution. In the end, remember that it's not how many friends someone has, but how strong their existing friendships are that really matters.

Student Page

Chapter 9: The Effects of Relationships on Your Mental Health

Human beings are designed to connect with other human beings. Everyone has **relationships** with a variety of people, whether that be friends at school and sports practice, family members in your immediate and extended family, or trusted adults from church, school, sports practice, etc. You are probably closer with some of these people than with others, but what matters is that you *are* connected with others. Research has shown that people who have a higher number of social connections are happier and experience fewer mental health struggles when compared to those who have fewer/weaker social connections. You may not pay much attention to the relationships in your life, but they all play a role in your behavior, physical and mental health, and risk of death.

Relationships impact your mental health because when people connect with each other, a hormone called **oxytocin** (one of the four happy hormones that was discussed in Chapter 4) is released throughout your body, which leaves you feeling happy, less stressed, and less lonely. Feelings of hopelessness (one of the main symptoms of depression and suicidal thoughts) are also decreased.

When a person does not have a lot of social connections, they tend to feel lonely, which can be dangerous. While connecting with others has the power to make one feel happy and content, **loneliness** has the power to disrupt sleep patterns, heighten anxiety and stress levels, and weaken the immune system. Furthermore, when someone is lonely for an extended period of time, it can lead to long-term health problems such as heart disease, stroke, and cancer. While diet, exercise, and sleep are all important aspects of a person's health, staying connected with friends, family, and the community also heavily contributes to living a healthy lifestyle.

While staying connected to others is important, if a relationship is abusive, negative, or toxic in any way, that can be more damaging to your mental health than being alone. **Negative relationships** can cause mental health problems like anxiety, depression, and the inability to trust other people. For this reason, it is important to distance yourself from these relationships if possible.

Sometimes, the negative relationship is with someone you cannot avoid, like a family member, for example. In this case, **conflict resolution** and **forgiveness** can be useful tools that will help you protect your mental health. However, if a relationship is **abusive**, steps need to be taken to leave the relationship and report the abuse to the proper authorities. This may involve telling a trusted person such as a parent, teacher, physician, or law enforcement officer.

One major benefit to being young is that you are constantly being exposed to new people through sports, clubs, and new classes. Take advantage of this unique opportunity, and make the first move if you want to make new friends! In the end, remember that it is not how many friends you have, but how strong your existing friendships are that really matters.

Chapter 9: The Effects of Relationships on Your Mental Health

How to Be a Good Friend

Be an Active Listener
Give your friend your undivided attention. Show you are listening by looking at your friend while they speak and putting your phone (or other distractions) away.

Be Trustworthy
When your friend tells you about his/her problems, do not gossip and tell others. Keep private information private. (Unless the person is in danger and the information should be shared with an adult.)

Support
Be there for and support each other when things are difficult just as much as when things are easy.

Apologize
Be ready and willing to take responsibility and apologize to your friend when you have wronged them or hurt their feelings, whether you meant to or not.

Embrace Your Differences
No two people are 100% alike; choose to embrace your differences! This happens when you feel comfortable being yourself around your friend, and they feel comfortable being themself around you.

Respect
Actively respect your friend by never judging them and always treating them with kindness.

Student Page

Chapter 9: The Effects of Relationships on Your Mental Health

Conflict Resolution Activity

Directions: Read the following scenario and act out the role-play with a partner to learn how to resolve conflict.

Rory tells Ben that she has a crush on Jordan. She wants this to be a secret, and Ben promises not to tell anyone. The next day at lunch, Rory is eating with her friend Brenna. Brenna says she heard multiple people talking about her crush on Jordan and that Jordan definitely knows now. Rory is embarrassed and knows this must mean that Ben broke her trust and told people her secret because she only told Ben. Rory is very upset by this and decides to confront Ben between classes.

Rory: Ben, can we talk in private about something?

Ben: Sure, let's step aside in the hallway.

Rory: Brenna told me that a lot of people know about my crush on Jordan. Why did you tell people when you promised me you wouldn't?

Ben: It's not that big of a deal. Everyone has crushes. Why are you so mad? You just need to get over it.

Rory: I'm mad because you broke your promise. I wanted to tell Jordan on my own but now he's heard this from other people besides me. When I tell you something in confidence and you promise not to repeat it, as my friend, I expect you to keep that promise. Can you try to understand where I'm coming from?

Ben: Jordan was going to find out one way or another. The way I see it, I did you a favor! I think you're overreacting.

Rory: An important part of being someone's friend is respecting their boundaries. I set a clear boundary to keep that information a secret. You promised not to tell anyone but broke your word and did anyway. I'm not mad. I'm just disappointed because I thought I could trust you.

Ben: It wouldn't have bothered me, so I guess I didn't think it would bother you either. Now that you have explained how you feel, I understand why you're upset. I will work on being more trustworthy. I'm sorry that I betrayed your trust and hurt your feelings. Can you forgive me?

Rory: Yes, I forgive you. Thank you for understanding! Let's head to class.

Parent/Teacher Page
Chapter 10: The Effects of Trauma on Your Mental Health

Children are among the most vulnerable in society and should be cared for and protected at all costs; however, research shows that more than two-thirds of children report that they have experienced at least one traumatic event by the time they are 16 years old. While children can be resilient, trauma can still have substantial and lasting impacts on their mental health. Research has shown that the earlier in life children are exposed to trauma, the more damaging it can be to them as they are still developing and learning how to cope with life's struggles.

A traumatic event could happen once, multiple times, or even over a long period. Trauma can affect a person's physical, psychological, social, emotional, and spiritual well-being, as well as their behaviors and ability to learn. Trauma is considered a risk factor for nearly all behavioral health and substance use disorders.

A common tool to measure trauma is the **ACEs survey**. ACEs stands for **Adverse Childhood Experiences** and are events that a child may experience that may be traumatic for them. An ACE could be something that happens to the child

A girl and her dog at an evacuation center after a wildfire.

(abuse, neglect, loss of a loved one, etc.) or something that happens in the child's environment (substance use or mental health problems, unstable living situation, etc.). This tool is helpful because many adults and children do not realize that what they have experienced is traumatic. The survey is intended for adults ages 18+ and can be found at the link below or by searching for "ACEs survey".

<https://www.acesaware.org/wp-content/uploads/2020/02/ACE-Questionnaire-for-Adults-Identified-English.pdf>

A traumatic event could be but is not limited to:
- Physical, sexual, or emotional abuse
- Neglect
- Witnessing or experiencing neighborhood, domestic, or school violence
- National disasters, terrorism, refugee or war experiences
- Serious accidents or life-threatening illness
- Sudden or violent loss of a loved one
- Military family-related stressors such as deployment, loss of a parent, injured parent, etc.

Statistics show that in 2019, approximately 1 in 5 high school students were bullied on school property, which does not include bullying that takes place at home or online. Furthermore, approximately 1 out of every 7 children experienced abuse and/or neglect in the last year, which is most likely an underestimate because many cases are not reported. Tragically, in 2019, 1,840 children died of abuse and neglect in the United States alone.

Parent/Teacher Page
Chapter 10: The Effects of Trauma on Your Mental Health

Trauma affects everyone differently, which means that everyone will have a different response to trauma. A trauma response can occur immediately or after some time and can be far-reaching, potentially affecting nearly every part of a person's well-being. Common trauma responses include:

- **Physical symptoms** such as long-term health problems like diabetes and heart disease
- **Emotional symptoms** such as emotional dysregulation or the inability to control big emotions, resulting in extreme behaviors and suspensions or expulsions at school
- **Relational symptoms** such as difficulty connecting with others, trusting others, and maintaining relationships
- **Mental health symptoms** such as increased likelihood of mental disorders like depression, anxiety, and PTSD
- **Developmental delays** resulting in the inability to learn new material in school at the same pace as their peers, delayed maturity, etc.

Trauma, though sometimes unavoidable, can also sometimes be prevented. As a parent, you have the power to provide a strong start for your child. It costs $0 to love, listen to, and respect your child. As a teacher, you have the power to notice when things are off in a child's life and report them. Many teachers shy away from reporting certain things to the child abuse hotline for fear of offending the family. However, it is always better to be safe than sorry, and reporting to a hotline could save a child's life. As a citizen, you have the power to advocate and vote for political leaders who will put economic and social support in place for families that need it (for example, policies that promote family-friendly work environments). You can raise awareness about ACEs. You can also advocate for a better society by setting an example of how to treat others. Finally, as an adult that a child trusts, you can teach them about safe dating, conflict resolution, and overall healthy relationship skills. You can also be a safe place for the child to talk about difficult subjects. Research shows that preventing adverse childhood experiences could have also prevented up to 1.9 million heart disease cases and 21 million depression cases.

For traumatic events that are not preventable, there are treatment and healing options available. Trauma-informed care is one of the most important things to look for when choosing a mental health provider. **Trauma-informed care** is when the provider has been trained (and is potentially credentialed) in treating individuals who have endured trauma. These providers are knowledgeable about the effects of trauma and the many resources available to help. If you are not sure how to find this kind of provider, you can ask the child's primary care physician for a referral. As you help the child seek help, remember to stay patient, as every child will recover at a different pace.

Student Page

Chapter 10: The Effects of Trauma on Your Mental Health

When a child experiences a traumatic event, it can stay with them for years to come. Research shows that more than two-thirds of children report that they have experienced at least one traumatic event by the time they are 16 years old. While children can heal and move on, trauma can still have substantial and lasting impacts on their mental health. In fact, the earlier in life children are exposed to trauma, the more damaging it can be to them as their brain is still developing and they are still learning healthy coping skills.

If you are unsure what trauma is, think of it this way—every person has an alarm system in their body. This alarm system works hard to keep you safe from danger by telling you to either fight or run away (this is commonly called the **fight or flight response**). **Trauma** is when something happens that triggers this alarm system and is too difficult to simply "get over" or cope with on your own. A traumatic event could happen once, multiple times, or even over a long period. Trauma can affect every part of a person's well-being, as well as their behaviors and ability to learn. Enduring trauma also often makes you more likely to suffer from behavioral health and substance use disorders.

A traumatic event could be but is not limited to:
- Physical, sexual, or emotional abuse
- Neglect
- Witnessing or experiencing neighborhood, domestic, or school violence
- National disasters, terrorism, refugee or war experiences
- Serious accidents or life-threatening illness
- Sudden or violent loss of a loved one
- Military family-related stressors such as deployment, loss of a parent, injured parent, etc.

Trauma affects everyone differently, which means that everyone will have a different response to trauma. A trauma response can occur immediately or after some time and can potentially affect nearly every part of a person's well-being. Common trauma responses include physical symptoms, emotional symptoms, relational symptoms, mental health symptoms, and developmental delays. For those who struggle with a traumatic event they have experienced, there are treatment and healing options available. Common treatment options that help those who are coping with trauma include therapy, medication, and coping skills that you know work for you. The following activity will help you identify common coping skills as healthy or unhealthy. You can learn more about coping skills in Chapter 13.

Chapter 10: The Effects of Trauma on Your Mental Health

Healthy and Unhealthy Coping Skills

There are many ways that people cope with the trauma they have experienced. The following is a list of coping skills that people often use to cope with trauma. Identify each as healthy or unhealthy by marking it with an H for healthy or a U for unhealthy.

For example –

__H__ *Meditation*

__U__ *Procrastination*

_____ 1. Practicing flexibility or yoga

_____ 2. Reacting with anger

_____ 3. Going for a walk to clear your head

_____ 4. Listening to calming music

_____ 5. Using drugs or alcohol

_____ 6. Using a grounding exercise

_____ 7. Skipping school

_____ 8. Participating in a creative outlet like drawing or journaling

_____ 9. Self-harm

_____ 10. Overeating or undereating

_____ 11. Destroying property

_____ 12. Temper tantrum

_____ 13. Talking to a therapist or counselor

_____ 14. Aggression or violence

_____ 15. Exercising

_____ 16. Name-calling or insulting others

_____ 17. Isolating yourself from others

_____ 18. Getting a good night's rest

_____ 19. Deep breathing exercises

_____ 20. Talking to a supportive friend or another adult

Parent/Teacher Page

Chapter 11: The Effects of Substance Use on Your Mental Health

At first thought, substance use may not seem like an issue that applies to adolescents, but by 12th grade, nearly two-thirds of students have tried alcohol at least once, and approximately half of high school students reported using marijuana at least once. Substance use may also not seem like a problem if it is done in controlled settings with supervision from an adult. However, substance use can have profound effects on the adolescent brain that is still developing and maturing, which can then impact their mental health. The **substances** we are talking about include anything from alcohol, cigarettes, and marijuana to cocaine, ecstasy, and methamphetamines, and they are all dangerous for a young person to consume in any amount.

Statistics show that substance use is a problem for many youths today. Alcohol, marijuana, and tobacco are the substances most used by adolescents, and people from 12 to 20 years old consume approximately one-tenth of all alcohol consumed in the United States. Further, 2 in 10 twelfth graders reported misusing prescription drugs, and 15% of high school students reported using illicit or injection drugs (cocaine, inhalants, heroin, methamphetamines, hallucinogens, or ecstasy).

Adolescence is a critical stage in a young person's life as they transition from a child to an adult and begin to experience growth spurts, puberty, and maturity. When an adolescent uses or abuses substances, this can affect their growth and development, especially their brain development. Drug use in youths is linked to concerning behaviors, such as the experience of and participation in violence and sexual risk behaviors. Substance use and misuse can lead to physical health problems in adulthood, such as heart disease, high blood pressure, and sleep disorders. And all these factors contribute to mental health and wellness, which is why substance use is also associated with mental health struggles and suicide risks.

Certain factors in a person's life put them more at risk of using substances, such as a family history of substance use, current parental substance use, associating with peers who use substances, struggling at school socially or academically, or enduring trauma.

If you suspect your teen is struggling with substance use, there are warning signs you can look for. If a teenager in your life is suddenly exhibiting behavior problems or is struggling with their grades or if they are being elusive about their whereabouts after school or on the weekends, substance use may be to blame. You can also look for physical symptoms, such as bloodshot eyes, runny nose, sore throat, or sudden weight loss, or if you notice that they are dizzy and having trouble remembering things. Check for physical evidence of drugs, alcohol, and other substances as well.

There are actions that can be taken to help prevent a young person from using substances, such as parental disapproval of substance use and educating the child on the dangers of substance use, parental monitoring of the child's whereabouts and friend groups, and being connected at school and home. If there is a teen in your life who may be using substances, you can educate them on the dangers and long-term effects of substance use. You can even have them take an at-home drug test. If a teen is addicted to one or more substances, there are treatment options available, such as cognitive behavioral therapy and aversion therapy, biological treatments like detoxification and antagonist drugs, as well as self-help groups (e.g., Alcoholics Anonymous, Narcotics Anonymous, etc.), and community prevention programs.

Chapter 11: The Effects of Substance Use on Your Mental Health

Research shows that many teens today use drugs regularly or experiment with them at least once. Adolescence is a critical time when children transition to adulthood, when they experience growth spurts and puberty, and when their brains continue to form and develop. Whether it be alcohol and vaping or cocaine and methamphetamines, all substances have a profound effect on a teenager's development and physical and mental well-being. Some **high-risk substances** can also leave the user with criminal charges and potential loss of life.

While vaping, marijuana, drinking, etc., may make you feel good in the moment, studies repeatedly show that substance use leads to an increased risk of mental health struggles like anxiety, depression, and suicide risks. Adolescent drug use is also linked to the experience of and participation in violence and sexual risk behaviors. Substance use in the teen years can also lead to physical health problems in adulthood, such as heart disease, high blood pressure, and sleep disorders.

Substance use often starts small and is a result of peer pressure. At times, it can feel like "everyone is doing it," but statistics and research show that is truly not the case. Use the following role-play activity to practice what to say when confronted with using drugs.

If you or someone you know is addicted to one or more substances, there are treatment options available, such as cognitive behavioral therapy and aversion therapy, biological treatments like detoxification and antagonist drugs, as well as self-help groups (e.g., Alcoholics Anonymous, Narcotics Anonymous, etc.), and community prevention programs.

Student Page

Chapter 11: The Effects of Substance Use on Your Mental Health

Substance Use Role Play Activity

Scenario 1 involves indirect peer pressure, seeing others use substances on social media and knowing you have access to the substance if you wanted. Divide the students into pairs. One student will play Student 1, and the other will play Student 2. Read the following script together.

Student 1: I found some weed in mom's bedroom last night, and I think I'm going to try some later.

Student 2: No, man. I don't think that would be good for you. Drugs are addictive and can really hurt you.

Student 1: I saw Mark talking about smoking on his social media, and it seems really fun. Plus, weed isn't addictive.

Student 2: That's actually not true. The National Institiute on Drug Abuse identifies marijuana as an addictive drug, and it is also considered a gateway drug that can quickly lead to much more dangerous substances.

Student 1: Well, my mom has a medical marijuana card, so it's legal.

Student 2: It might be legal for your mom to consume controlled amounts of marijuana due to a serious illness, but your brain and body are still developing, and marijuana can have bad effects on how your brain and body develop.

Student 1: Oh, come on. What can one time hurt? I'll share it with you if that's what you're worried about!

Student 2: Just trust me. My cousin messed around with that stuff, and it nearly ruined his life. Plus, we could both get kicked off the team for doing that.

Student 1: You're right. I'll leave it alone and tell my mom to put it in a different, more secure location so I can't find it again.

Student Page

Chapter 11: The Effects of Substance Use on Your Mental Health

Substance Use Role Play Activity

Scenario 2 involves direct peer pressure from a friend or older sibling. Divide the students into pairs. One student will play Student 1, and the other will play Student 2. Read the following script together.

Student 1: Have you ever tried vaping?

Student 2: No, I haven't.

Student 1: You should! It's dope, and you can even get different flavors.

Student 2: No, thanks! Drugs are bad for your body and mind, and I don't think that's something I ever want to do.

Student 1: Aw, come on! Just try it one time. One time can't hurt, right?

Student 2: Drugs can keep you from thinking clearly, which can lead to making poor decisions and not doing well in school. Please respect my decision to say no.

Student 1: It's not hardcore drugs, it's just vaping. Everyone does it. Don't be such a loser.

Student 2: I just don't think that stuff is worth my time. I have things I want to accomplish in life, and I don't want drugs to get in the way.

List five reasons to avoid using drugs.

1. _____
2. _____
3. _____
4. _____
5. _____

List five things you could do instead of using drugs.

1. _____
2. _____
3. _____
4. _____
5. _____

Parent/Teacher Page

Chapter 12: Treating Mental Disorders: Therapy, Medication, and Other Professional Treatment Options

When a teen has been diagnosed with a mental disorder, it is important to be aware of the various treatment options that are available to help them. There are multiple professional treatment options that have been proven to be effective for those struggling with a mental disorder. As always, it is necessary that these treatment methods are provided by a mental health professional. Professional treatment options include:

- **Therapy**, when conducted by a trained mental health professional, will enable the patient to explore their thoughts, feelings, and behaviors while aiming to improve their mental health symptoms, problematic behaviors, and overall well-being.

- **Medication**, when prescribed by a psychiatrist, can be helpful to many adolescents struggling with mental health. Medication does not cure mental disorders but can help manage the symptoms that a person experiences. Medication is commonly paired with therapy for maximum effectiveness.

- **Hospitalization** is an option that provides safety for children, adolescents, and adults who may pose a threat to themselves or others. While hospitalized, the residents are connected with multiple resources—psychiatry, counseling in a one-on-one setting, counseling in a group or family setting, and other group activities to assist in stabilization.

- **Support groups and peer support.** A support group is when the members are all working toward a shared goal and spur one another on. Peer support is when a person discusses their mental health issues with another person who has experienced similar struggles.

- **Complementary and alternative medicine** is not considered standard medical care but is a growing movement. This method involves taking herbal supplements, drinking certain herbal teas, eating certain foods or following certain diets, acupuncture, massage, and chiropractic care.

- A **self-help plan** is an intentional and specific list of coping strategies that a person knows works for them. This list may constantly evolve as a person grows and changes and can be helpful with symptom management.

If you believe that a teen in your life could benefit from one of these treatment options, a quick Google search can list the options available to you in your area. In some instances, it may be necessary for the child to see their primary care physician first to obtain a referral. If the teen is needing immediate help, call 911 or the free and confidential mental health crisis lifeline by dialing or texting 988.

Chapter 12: Treating Mental Disorders: Therapy, Medication, and Other Professional Treatment Options

When treating mental disorders, there are multiple professional treatment options that have been proven to be effective. Professional treatment options include:

- **Therapy and counseling**, when conducted by a trained mental health professional, will enable the patient to explore their thoughts, feelings, and behaviors while aiming to improve their mental health symptoms, problematic behaviors, and overall well-being.

- **Medication**, when prescribed by a psychiatrist, can be helpful to many adolescents struggling with mental health. Medication does not cure mental disorders but can help manage the symptoms that a person experiences. Medication is commonly paired with therapy for maximum effectiveness.

Equine therapy uses horses to help treat a number of disorders.

- **Hospitalization** is an option that provides safety for children, adolescents, and adults who may pose a threat to themselves or others. While hospitalized, the residents are connected with multiple resources—psychiatry, counseling in a one-on-one setting, counseling in a group or family setting, and other group activities to assist in stabilization.

- **Support groups and peer support.** A support group is when the members are all working toward a shared goal and spur one another on. Peer support is when a person discusses their mental health issues with another person who has experienced similar struggles.

- **Complementary and alternative medicine** is not considered standard medical care but is a growing movement. This method involves taking herbal supplements, drinking certain herbal teas, eating certain foods or following certain diets, acupuncture, massage, and chiropractic care.

- **Self-help plan.** This is an intentional and specific list of coping strategies that a person knows works for them. This list may constantly evolve as a person grows and changes and can be helpful with symptom management. See pages 57–58 for a list of coping skills.

If you think you may benefit from one of the previous treatment options, talk with a trusted adult (parent, doctor, teacher, coach, pastor, etc.) about the treatment option(s) you think you may need, and they can help you get connected. If you need immediate help and think you may be a harm to yourself or others, call 911 or the free and confidential mental health crisis lifeline by dialing or texting 988.

Chapter 12: Treating Mental Disorders: Therapy, Medication, and Other Professional Treatment Options

Treatment Planning Activity

Scenario 1:

Your friend Megan tells you that her father has recently passed away. Megan no longer wants to hang out on the weekends, and she wants to be alone in her room all weekend instead. She zones out in class, has started doing poorly on quizzes and tests, and sometimes she doesn't come to school at all. Megan barely eats at lunch and says she isn't hungry. You notice that Megan hardly smiles anymore, and you also see her come out of the bathroom crying a few times. She tells you that she doesn't see how life can get any better without her dad and that she wishes she had a different life.

With a partner, discuss what combination of treatment options you think would be helpful for Megan, explain why, and how she would go about accessing the necessary treatment.

Scenario 2:

You notice that your friend Kyle seems to be quite anxious lately. He has a hard time relaxing and is constantly worried about something, whether he is overthinking something in the past or fearing the worst will happen in the future. He tells you that he doesn't think he fits in very well at school even though he really wants everyone to like him. The English assignment that you were both given took him twice the amount of time it took you to complete because he kept redoing parts of it when he didn't think it was good enough. He has also been complaining about stomachaches and how he has a hard time sleeping; sometimes this even causes him to miss school.

With a partner, discuss what combination of treatment options you think would be helpful for Kyle, explain why, and how he would go about accessing the necessary treatment.

Disclaimer: Remember that it is not your responsibility to "fix" your friends. In real life, you should not be making treatment plans for your friends, as this should be left to adult professionals only. This treatment planning activity is for learning purposes only.

Parent/Teacher Page

Chapter 13: Treating Mental Disorders: Coping Skills

Coping skills are a crucial part of life, as they help people navigate everyday stressors. There are many stressors in the teenage years, such as a big test or presentation, having a hard conversation with someone, trying out for a sport, worrying about what other people think, overcoming peer pressure, etc. There are 100+ different strategies that can be utilized to help cope with difficult situations.

Don't wait until you feel better to do something,
do something to make yourself feel better.

Coping skills can be divided into categories, and this is helpful because at different times, teens will need support in different ways. When you begin to learn what kind of support is needed in the moment, take a moment to reflect and choose a coping skill from the necessary category. The more you and your teen practice this, the easier it will be to employ when needed.

Common coping skills categories and examples of each can be found below.

- **Rest and relaxation.** This is an activity that helps you feel calm, lowers your heart rate, and eases the tension in your muscles. Examples include taking a nap, going to bed early, lying down in a dark room, or foam rolling your muscles after a workout.

- **Companionship.** This is an activity that helps you feel connected with others. An example of this is calling a friend to process a stressful event.

- **Health.** This is an activity that benefits your physical health. Examples include eating a healthy meal, exercising, getting enough sleep, limiting caffeine intake, avoiding alcohol and drugs, etc.

- **Distraction.** This is a healthy activity that takes your mind off the current stressful situation. Examples include puzzles, books, crafts, or positive music and movies.

- **Opposite action.** This is an activity that is the opposite of your impulse that will leave you feeling positive. Examples include watching a funny movie, listening to a motivational speech, listing self-affirmations, etc.

Drawing or other art activities can provide a distraction and a way to express one's feelings.

- **Emotional awareness.** This is an activity that helps you identify and express your feelings. Examples include journaling or drawing to identify and express your feelings.

Parent/Teacher Page

Chapter 13: Treating Mental Disorders: Coping Skills

- **Mindfulness.** This is an activity that will center and ground you in the present moment. Examples include meditation, deep breathing exercises, and the 5 senses exercise.
  - The **5 senses exercise** is a grounding activity you can do where you name five things you can see, four things you can touch, three things you can hear, two things you can smell, and one thing you can taste.

- **Spirituality.** This is an activity that helps you feel connected to your spirit and/or the spirit of a higher power. Examples include praying, meditating, and enjoying time in nature.

- **Crisis Plan.** This is a list of contact information and supports that you can lean on when coping skills are not enough. Examples of this include the mental health crisis hotline number and the name and number of trusted individuals who can support you—your mentor, therapist, psychiatrist, etc.

Mindfulness and spirituality can help keep a person calm and centered.

Coping skills are helpful when they are used as part of a larger treatment plan that includes therapy and medication, or when they are used to simply make it through a bad day. However, while coping skills can help with symptom management, they should not be relied upon as the only source of long-term treatment if the person has a diagnosed mental disorder or has life-disrupting symptoms that last for more than two consistent weeks. For long-term treatment options, see the previous chapter.

There are also unhealthy coping skills to be aware of, which are things that might provide quick relief but will create bigger problems down the road. An unhealthy coping skill could be driving fast in a car, slamming doors, using substances, chewing fingernails, being aggressive or violent, over or undereating, yelling at friends or family, or avoiding friends and family.

In addition to coping skills, self-care should also be a regular part of the person's daily routine. While coping skills help a person minimize and endure stressful situations, **self-care** is when the person does something that they enjoy or is calming, regardless of how they feel at the time. Self-care can help prevent feelings of stress and anxiety, improve concentration and energy throughout the day, and leave a person feeling generally happy. Encourage your teen to do relaxing and/or enjoyable things for themselves every day, or as often as possible, to help protect their mental well-being.

Student Page

Chapter 13: Treating Mental Disorders: Coping Skills

There are many stressful situations that a teenager encounters, such as a big test or presentation, having a hard conversation with someone, trying out for a sport, worrying about what other people think of you, overcoming peer pressure, etc. **Coping skills** are things you can do to help yourself calm down when you experience something stressful. It's important to do something to make yourself feel better, instead of waiting until you feel better to do something.

Coping skills can be divided into categories, which is helpful because at different times you will need support in different ways. When you begin to learn what kind of support you need in a situation, take a moment to reflect and choose a coping skill from the necessary category. The more you practice this, the easier it will be to do. Common coping skills categories are listed below.

- **Rest and relaxation**—an activity that helps you feel calm, lowers your heart rate, and eases the tension in your muscles
- **Companionship**—an activity that helps you feel connected with others
- **Health**—an activity that benefits your physical health
- **Distraction**—a healthy activity that takes your mind off the current stressful situation
- **Opposite action**—an activity that is the opposite of your impulse that will leave you feeling positive
- **Emotional awareness**—an activity that helps you identify and express your feelings
- **Mindfulness**—an activity that will center and ground you in the present moment
- **Spirituality**—an activity that helps you feel connected to your spirit and/or the spirit of a higher power
- **Crisis plan**—a list of contact information and supports that you can lean on when coping skills are not enough

Coping skills are helpful when they are used as part of a larger treatment plan that includes therapy and medication, or when they are used to simply make it through a bad day. Coping skills can help with symptoms of stress, but if you have been diagnosed with a mental disorder, you will need to utilize one or more of the treatment options listed in the previous chapter. Talk with a trusted adult if you think you need access to a professional treatment option.

In addition to coping skills, self-care should also be a regular part of your daily routine. While coping skills help you minimize and endure stressful situations, **self-care** is when you do something that you enjoy or is calming, regardless of how you feel at the time. Self-care can help prevent feelings of stress and anxiety, improve concentration and energy throughout the day, and leave you feeling generally happy. Try to do something relaxing and/or enjoyable every day, or as often as possible, to help protect your mental well-being. If you have a smartphone, you can search "coping skills" or "self-care" in the app store and you will find many free apps that help you plan and schedule self-care, as well as create and maintain daily routines.

In the following Personal Coping Skills Chart on page 59, use the definition and examples listed in each coping skills category to think of and list your own examples within that category. You may use the List of 107 Coping Skills to help you think, and the example that is already listed may also be one of the coping skills you choose. By the end, you should have a list of coping skills in each category that you know will work for you.

Chapter 13: Treating Mental Disorders: Coping Skills

List of 107 Coping Skills

1. Read a book.
2. Hang out with your friends.
3. Create origami or paper airplanes.
4. Kick, bounce, or throw a ball.
5. Cry.
6. Do something kind for someone.
7. Go for a walk.
8. Spend time alone in the quiet.
9. Paint your nails.
10. Declutter.
11. Meal plan/prep.
12. Read a joke book.
13. Plan a trip you'd like to take.
14. Eat your favorite food.
15. Write a poem.
16. Identify your emotions.
17. Take up a new hobby.
18. Count to 100.
19. Play sports.
20. Express your feelings to someone.
21. Take a nap.
22. Paint.
23. Draw a picture.
24. Make a craft.
25. Create a new morning or bedtime routine.
26. Take a bath or shower.
27. Draw cartoons.
28. Drink cold water.
29. Drink hot tea.
30. Make a list of everything you need to do.
31. Diffuse or apply essential oils.
32. Create goals for the future.
33. Take a break.
34. Watch your favorite movie.
35. Tell someone you're thankful for them.
36. Watch a movie that will make you laugh.
37. Organize something.
38. Play a card game.
39. Journal.
40. Stand up and stretch.
41. Compliment yourself.
42. Laugh.
43. Write a letter to someone (even if you don't send it).
44. Learn a magic trick.
45. Close your eyes and relax.
46. List 10 things you like about yourself.
47. Try a new recipe.
48. Chew gum.
49. Read inspirational quotes.
50. Read the Bible.
51. Go for a walk.
52. Build something.
53. Make a gratitude list.

Chapter 13: Treating Mental Disorders: Coping Skills

List of 107 Coping Skills

54. Clean something.
55. Go for a bike ride.
56. Doodle on paper.
57. Hum your favorite song.
58. Call a friend.
59. Squeeze a stress ball.
60. Look at pictures you've taken.
61. Write a short story.
62. Say "I can do this" 10 times.
63. Pray.
64. Visualize your favorite place.
65. Think of a happy memory.
66. Think about someone you love.
67. Get enough sleep.
68. Jog in place.
69. Practice yoga.
70. Rip paper into little pieces.
71. Write a list.
72. Take pictures.
73. Learn a new instrument.
74. Blow bubbles.
75. Schedule time for self-care.
76. Learn a new song on your instrument.
77. Use a relaxation app.
78. Do schoolwork.
79. Rearrange your room.
80. Use a guided meditation app.
81. Paint with watercolors.

82. Teach your pet a trick.
83. Practice positive self-talk.
84. Play a video game.
85. Pet an animal.
86. Talk to a counselor.
87. Watch something funny.
88. Eat a healthy meal.
89. Spend time with family.
90. Go for a hike.
91. Take deep breaths.
92. Face your problem.
93. Do a puzzle.
94. Volunteer your time.
95. Play a board game.
96. Play a game outside.
97. Go to the park.
98. Meet someone new.
99. Smile until you feel better.
100. Do yardwork.
101. Talk in a funny voice.
102. Try to make someone laugh.
103. Sing.
104. Write your own song.
105. Plan an outfit for tomorrow.
106. Sew, weave, knit, or crochet.
107. Read this whole list!

Student Page

Chapter 13: Treating Mental Disorders: Coping Skills

Personal Coping Skills Chart

Rest and Relaxation	Companionship	Health	Distraction	Opposite Action
An activity that helps you feel calm, lowers your heart rate, and eases the tension in your muscles	An activity that helps you feel connected to loved ones	An activity that benefits your physical health	An activity that takes your mind off the current stressful situation	An activity that is the opposite of your impulse that will leave you feeling positive
Example: take a nap	**Example:** call a friend to talk about how your days are going	**Example:** go for a walk	**Example:** put together a puzzle	**Example:** watch a funny video
Student's examples:	Student's examples:	Student's examples:	Student's examples:	Student's examples:

Emotional Awareness	Mindfulness	Spirituality	Crisis Plan
An activity that helps you identify and express your feelings	An activity that will center and ground you in the present moment	An activity that helps you feel connected to your spirit and/or the spirit of a higher power	A list of contact information and supports for when coping skills are not enough
Example: journaling with a prompt	**Example:** deep breathing exercises	**Example:** pray	**Example:** suicide and mental health crisis hotline at 988
Student's examples:	Student's examples:	Student's examples:	Student's examples:

Answer Key

What Is Mental Health: How Am I Feeling Today? (p. 4–5)
Answers will vary.

Communicating with Others About Your Mental Health: Talking About Mental Health (p. 7–8)
Scenario 1:
Should you talk to someone about how you are feeling?
Yes.
Name of trusted person and what you would say to them: Answers will vary.
Scenario 2:
Does this scenario require action? Yes.
Should you involve an adult? Yes.
Name of trusted person and what you would say to them: Answers will vary.
Scenario 3:
Does this scenario require action? No.
Should you involve an adult? No.
What should you say to your friend? Answers will vary.

Common Mental Disorders: Matching Activity (p. 13)
1. D   2. C   3. B   4. E
5. A

The Connection of the Body and Mind: Fill in the Blank Activity (p. 15)
In the following order: brain, mind, messages, hormones, pituitary gland, connection, happy, dopamine/endorphins, endorphins/dopamine, adrenaline/cortisol, cortisol/adrenaline.

The Effects of Food on Your Mental Health: Food Diary and Goal Food Diary (p. 22–23)
Answers will vary.

The Effects of Exercise on Your Mental Health: Incorporating Exercise Into Your Daily Routine (p. 26)
Answers will vary.

The Effects of Rest on Your Mental Health: Worksheet and Sleep Diary (p. 31–32)
Answers will vary.

The Effects of Social Media on Your Mental Health: Social Media Detox Activity (p. 37)
Answers will vary.

The Effects of Trauma on Your Mental Health: Healthy and Unhealthy Coping Skills (p. 46)
1. H   2. U   3. H   4. H

5. U   6. H   7. U   8. H
9. U   10. U   11. U   12. U
13. H   14. U   15. H   16. U
17. U   18. H   19. H   20. H

The Effects of Substance Use on Your Mental Health: Substance Use Role Play Activity (p. 50)
Answers will vary.

Treating Mental Disorders: Therapy, ...: Treatment Planning Activity (p. 53)
Scenario 1:
Megan has depression. She should pursue counseling or therapy and possibly consult a psychiatrist to discuss medication if her symptoms last more than two weeks, as they are already disrupting her daily life (i.e., doing poorly on quizzes and tests and decreasing appetite). Grief support groups and peer support would encourage Megan and help her feel less alone. Alternative medicine and a self-help plan may also be beneficial for Megan as they could help manage her symptoms and her ability to cope. Hospitalization would not be necessary.

How to access various sources in your specific area will vary but can commonly begin with a simple Google search.
Scenario 2:
Kyle has anxiety. He should pursue counseling or therapy and possibly consult a psychiatrist to discuss medication if his symptoms last more than two weeks, as they are already disrupting his daily life (i.e., homework takes him an unreasonable amount of time, he suffers from stomachaches and inability to sleep, and sometimes misses school). Support groups where Kyle can learn how to manage his anxiety alongside others may be helpful, and having a friend he can go to that has also experienced anxiety will encourage him and help him feel less alone. Alternative medicine may help to manage symptoms (e.g., drinking chamomile tea before bed could help him sleep), and a self-help plan with coping skills that work for Kyle may help ease his stomachaches and allow him to make it to school even when he is anxious about attending. Hospitalization would not be necessary.

How to access various sources in your specific area will vary but can commonly begin with a simple Google search.

Treating Mental Disorders: Coping Skills: Personal Coping Skills Chart (p. 59)
Answers will vary.

Bibliography

Bashir, Hilal, and Shabir A Bhat. "Effects of Social Media on Mental Health: A Review." *International Journal of Indian Psychology,* vol. 4, no. 3, 30 June 2017, <https://doi.org/10.25215/0403.134>.

Bauer, Brent A. "Pros and Cons of Melatonin." *Mayo Clinic,* Mayo Foundation for Medical Education and Research, 13 Nov. 2020, <https://www.mayoclinic.org/healthy-lifestyle/adult-health/expert-answers/melatonin-side-effects/faq-20057874>.

Better Health Channel Staff. "Strong Relationships, Strong Health." *Better Health Channel,* 24 Feb. 2022, <https://www.betterhealth.vic.gov.au/health/healthyliving/strong-relationships-strong-health>.

Cafasso, Jacquelyn. "Adrenaline Rush: Everything You Should Know." *Healthline,* Healthline Media, 1 Nov. 2018, <https://www.healthline.com/health/adrenaline-rush#causes>.

CDC Staff. "Anxiety and Depression in Children: Get the Facts." *Centers for Disease Control and Prevention,* Centers for Disease Control and Prevention, 13 Apr. 2022, <https://www.cdc.gov/childrensmentalhealth/features/anxiety-depression-children.html>.

CDC Staff. "Teen Substance Use & Risks." *Centers for Disease Control and Prevention,* Centers for Disease Control and Prevention, 10 Feb. 2020, <https://www.cdc.gov/ncbddd/fasd/features/teen-substance-use.html>.

CDC Staff. "Preventing Adverse Childhood Experiences: Data to Action (PACE:D2A)." *Centers for Disease Control and Prevention,* Centers for Disease Control and Prevention, 19 Aug. 2021, <https://www.cdc.gov/violenceprevention/aces/preventingace-datatoaction.html>.

Centers for Disease Control and Prevention (2019). *Preventing Adverse Childhood Experiences: Leveraging the Best Available Evidence.* Atlanta, GA: Division of Violence Prevention, National Center for Injury Prevention and Control, Centers for Disease Control and Prevention. <https://www.cdc.gov/violenceprevention/pdf/preventingACEs.pdf>

"Common Sleep Problems." Edited by Mary L. Gavin, *KidsHealth,* The Nemours Foundation, June 2020, <https://kidshealth.org/en/teens/sleep.html>.

Comer, Ronald J. *Fundamentals of Abnormal Psychology.* 8th ed., Worth Publishers, 2016.

DoSomething.org, Staff. "11 Facts About Mental Health." *DoSomething.org,* 2021, <https://www.dosomething.org/us/facts/11-facts-about-mental-health>.

Ellis, Esther. "How Many Calories Does My Teen Need?" *EatRight,* 4 Oct. 2019, <https://www.eatright.org/food/nutrition/dietary-guidelines-and-myplate/how-many-calories-does-my-teen-need>.

Elmaghraby, Rana, and Stephanie Garayalde. "What Is ADHD?" *Psychiatry.org - What Is ADHD?,* American Psychiatric Association, June 2022, <https://www.psychiatry.org/patients-families/adhd/what-is-adhd>.

Hart, Patricia. "What Is the Mind-Body Connection?" *Taking Charge of Your Health & Wellbeing,* 2016, <https://www.takingcharge.csh.umn.edu/what-is-the-mind-body-connection>.

Hentzel, Clayton, director. *Glowing Rectangles,* The Crossing, 20 Mar. 2022, <https://www.youtube.com/watch?v=sRQA6WoZ2ZM&list=PLwXQlDmeS2gbNSmY_gDKl_6ql85LFo2ax&index=6>. Accessed 7 July 2022.

Lonergan, Alexandra R., et al. "Protect Me from My Selfie: Examining the Association between Photo-Based Social Media Behaviors and Self-Reported Eating Disorders in Adolescence." *International Journal of Eating Disorders,* vol. 53, no. 5, 7 Apr. 2020, pp. 755–766., <https://doi.org/10.1002/eat.23256>.

Marzilli, Eleonora, et al. "A Narrative Review of Binge Eating Disorder in Adolescence: Prevalence, Impact, and Psychological Treatment Strategies." *Adolescent Health, Medicine and Therapeutics,* vol. 9, 5 Jan. 2018, pp. 17–30., <https://doi.org/10.2147/AHMT.S148050>.

Mayo Clinic Staff. "Depression (Major Depressive Disorder)." *Mayo Clinic,* Mayo Foundation for Medical Education and Research, 3 Feb. 2018, <https://www.mayoclinic.org/diseases-conditions/depression/symptoms-causes/syc-20356007>.

Bibliography

Mayo Clinic Staff. "How to Help Your Teen Navigate Social Media." *Mayo Clinic,* Mayo Foundation for Medical Education and Research, 26 Feb. 2022, <https://www.mayoclinic.org/healthy-lifestyle/tween-and-teen-health/in-depth/teens-and-social-media-use/art-20474437>.

MedlinePlus Staff. "Hyperactivity: MedlinePlus Medical Encyclopedia." *MedlinePlus,* U.S. National Library of Medicine, 27 May 2020, <https://medlineplus.gov/ency/article/003256.htm>.

Mentalhealth.gov Staff. "What Is Mental Health?" *What Is Mental Health? I MentalHealth.gov,* U.S. Department of Health and Human Services, 2021, <https://www.mentalhealth.gov/basics/what-is-mental-health>.

Mental Health Foundation Staff. "Relationships and Community: Statistics." *Mental Health Foundation,* 2022, <https://mentalhealth.org.uk/explore-mental-health/statistics/relationships-community-statistics>.

MHA Staff. "Mental Health Treatments." *Mental Health America,* 2022, <https://mhanational.org/mental-health-treatments>.

NIMH Staff. "Major Depression." *National Institute of Mental Health,* U.S. Department of Health and Human Services, Jan. 2022, <https://www.nimh.nih.gov/health/statistics/major-depression>.

Owens, Alexandra. "Oxytocin: What It Is, How It Makes You Feel & Why It Matters." *Psycom,* 23 Sept. 2021, <https://www.psycom.net/oxytocin>.

Paschke, Kerstin, et al. "ICD-11-Based Assessment of Social Media Use Disorder in Adolescents: Development and Validation of the Social Media Use Disorder Scale for Adolescents." *Frontiers in Psychiatry,* vol. 12, 22 Apr. 2021, <https://doi.org/10.3389/fpsyt.2021.661483>.

Ramsey, Drew. *Eat to Beat Depression and Anxiety.* First ed., HarperCollins, 2021.

Raypole, Crystal. "Happy Hormones: What They Are and How to Boost Them." *Healthline,* Healthline Media, 26 July 2022, <https://www.healthline.com/health/happy-hormone#meditation>.

SAMHSA Staff. "Understanding Child Trauma." *Substance Abuse and Mental Health Services Administration,* 2022, <https://www.samhsa.gov/child-trauma/understanding-child-trauma>.

Torres, Felix. "What Is Posttraumatic Stress Disorder (PTSD)?" *American Psychiatric Association,* Aug. 2020, <https://psychiatry.org/patients-families/ptsd/what-is-ptsd>.

Varma, Prerna, et al. "Younger People Are More Vulnerable to Stress, Anxiety and Depression during COVID-19 Pandemic: A Global Cross-Sectional Survey." *Progress in Neuro-Psychopharmacology and Biological Psychiatry,* vol. 109, 26 Dec. 2020, <https://doi.org/10.1016/j.pnpbp.2020.110236>.

VA Staff. "PTSD: National Center for PTSD." *U.S. Department of Veterans Affairs,* 18 Sept. 2018, <https://www.ptsd.va.gov/understand/common/common_children_teens.asp>.

Walker, Matthew. *Why We Sleep.* Simon & Schuster, 2017.

Your Hormones Staff. "Pituitary Gland." *You and Your Hormones,* 2022, <https://www.yourhormones.info/glands/pituitary-gland/>.

Zochil, Marina L., and Einar B. Thorsteinsson. "Exploring Poor Sleep, Mental Health, and Help-Seeking Intention in University Students." *Australian Journal of Psychology,* vol. 70, no. 1, 2018, pp. 41–47., <https://doi.org/10.1111/AJPY.12160>.